Believe

GERALD M. ALLEN

ISBN 979-8-89130-669-1 (paperback)
ISBN 979-8-89130-670-7 (digital)

Copyright © 2024 by Gerald M. Allen

All rights reserved. No part of this publication may be reproduced, distributed, or transmitted in any form or by any means, including photocopying, recording, or other electronic or mechanical methods without the prior written permission of the publisher. For permission requests, solicit the publisher via the address below.

Christian Faith Publishing
832 Park Avenue
Meadville, PA 16335
www.christianfaithpublishing.com

Printed in the United States of America

My lips proclaim the glory
Of my Lord, the Risen King,
My eyes receive His guiding light
With joyous love my heart to
Him does sing.

I wish to dedicate the poems in this book to my loving wife, Ronnie, whom Father God called home to be with Him.

Dedication

I would like to dedicate this book
With a special little rhyme,
To the gift the Father gave to me
Four loving daughters that are mine.

First there came Evelyn Jean
And then the second Cathy Lynn,
The third then came Ronda Lee
Then last the baby Tracy Ann.

When they were just small babies
As they laid there in their cribs,
In my mind there still I see them
Thank you, God, for my daughters that you give.

Though they be no longer babies
But in my heart they are you see,
And I thank you, God my Father,
For these Blessings you gave me.

God Bless and keep you my children.

Dedication

I dedicate this book to my Lord and Savior Jesus Christ.

Through all the words be written
Through my hand; be sure that it
Is the prompting of the Spirit that guides these words!

Contents

Introduction xvii

Welcome Home 1
Praise to Jesus 3
A New Path 5
The Spirit 7
Reflections 9
Old Mother Hubbard 10
How Amazing All This Is 11
Empty Vessel Made of Clay 13
Get Out of that Ditch 14
I Wonder 16
Happy Birthday, Jesus 17
A Letter to Mary 19
Humility 21
Our Dearest Friend 23
Teach and Serve 25
In Christ My Love 26
Rolled Away 27
Look Up 29
Lord God My Everything 31
God First 33
Always There 34
Cleansing Blood 36
Temptation 38
Open Up Your Door 40
He Comforts Me 42
Your Plan 43
Go There Every Day 45

Little Bits of Heaven	46
Our Light	48
Awaken Me	49
Just a Limb	50
Little Child of God	51
Your Day with Jesus	53
Jesus Saved Me	55
God Time	57
Trinity	59
Then and Now	60
The Glory Road	61
Who	63
My Love, My Wife, My Ronnie	65
Blood of Love	67
Lord Jesus and Me	69
Angels That Do Fly	71
Meet My Friend Lord Jesus	73
Thanks Be to God	75
Christmas Is!	77
Worship Invitation	79
Gift	80
A Beautiful World	81
He's	82
Friends	84
Instructions	86
A Day with Jesus	88
Better Way	90
I Believe	92
Problem Solved	93
How Heavenly	94
Guide My Words	95
Sing Praise	96
Thank You	97
Closing Thought	98
Across the Jordan to Many Treasures	99
All Praise	100

Almighty Power, All Caring Love	101
Are You Ready?	103
A Matter of Life	104
Attentive	105
A Special Day	107
Beauty	109
Christ Our Gift	111
Crucified	113
Do Good	115
A Time of Giving	116
Forever the Word	117
Forever with Jesus	119
God's Physician	120
God's Word! New Day! Same Way!	121
Guidance	123
Healing Well	124
How a Poem!	125
I Walk on His Path	126
Intercede	127
Jesus Love Prayer	129
Lead Me	130
Love, Attention, and Praise	131
Mirror, Mirror	133
My Bride	135
My God	136
My God, My Jesus, My Spirit	137
My Prayer	139
Look to the Scriptures	140
My Talk with Jesus	141
Never-Ending Thank You	143
On Calvary	145
Only This Day	147
Perfect Love	148
Promised Land	149
Pure Love	150
Received	151

Return	152
Sacrifice	153
Sister Mary Rose McGeady	155
Speck of Life	156
The Sabbath	157
The Seed	159
The Trumpets Call	160
The Water's Edge	161
Those of Need	163
To Jesus	164
Trouble in Lust	165
Up from the Valley	166
What a Day	167
Why Man? Why Woman?	168
With God a New Day	169
The Door	170
With God's Help!	171
Your Word	173
Loving God	174
Give Me God's Word	175
The Evil Spirit Antichrist	176
For All to See	179
His Word	180
The Body of Life	181
Jonah	182
A Special Place	185
J. E. S. U. S.	186
A Leaf! A Life!	187
Birthday Gift	188
Through Life's Storms	189
Prayer for Julie	190
Prayer for Barb	192
Three in One	193
If Not for God	194
Guard Your Mouth	196
From His Cross Love	197

From My Heart	198
Love and Glory	199
A Wish?	200
The Cup of Life	202
For My Great Grandsons	203
Born Again	204
Let It Be Love!	206
Shared Burden	207
On Thy Cross	208
With Jesus	209
A New Start	210
Glory, Love, and Life	211
From Him	212
Lead Your Heart to Love	213
This I See	214
Climb Your Hill	215
Love	216
My Cost	217
A Helping Hand	219
Worry	220
Given	221
A Path to God's Garden	222
The Son	224
Star Bright	226
Message	227
Be My God	228
Three Equals One	229
Always There for Me	230
The Miracle of a Raindrop	231
Talk	232
For the Joy of a Child	233
Early Morning Call	234
Listen	235
At the Cross	236
Great Will Be the Day	237
Compassion	238

Light	239
In Dark Be Light	240
Three Be	241
Symphony	242
Jesus the Only Way	243
Fixed Goal	244
A Blessed Day from Heaven	245
Redeeming Salvation	246
A Baby Boy	247
A Place to Rest	248
A Prayer for All	249
Heavenly Light	250
Jesus Christ Be the Glory	251
It Is God's Love	252
When? God's Will!	253
Little Things	254
Trials	256
A Closing Thought	259
Acknowledgements	261

Introduction

As a man of seventy-four years of age and having been married to the love of my life for fifty-two and a half years, my world was shaken when my love, Ronnie, was stricken with lung cancer in 2008. I remember the dreadful feeling of losing her after we had spent a lifetime together.

Through it all, she remained strong with her belief in our Lord and Savior Jesus Christ. When times were hard for me to understand not being able to help her, she would comfort me. She told me she knew she was in God's hands and was right where He wanted her to be.

Living all my life, I believed there is a God and Jesus is His Son, but I had never been baptized. Ronnie made me promise to be baptized. Before she died, we had a pastor come to the house, and he baptized me.

I lost her on September 26, 2010.

Moving through the next couple years without my Ronnie and not being a religious person, more and more I realized there was something missing from my life. Not just my Ronnie but something much greater. Her faith in God our Father, God the Son, and God the Holy Spirit.

As the song goes, "Count your blessings, name them one by one…" I began to see there were some undesirable things in my early childhood the Lord my God had brought me through.

God brought Ronnie and I together when I was eighteen years old and she was sixteen years old. We began our life together filled with blessing after blessing.

Were there some rough, hard times? Absolutely! But there, once again, I now see how the Hand of God brought us through those tough times.

We were given four special blessings, four loving daughters, and through the love of God, my daughters brought forth eight more blessings. And thus far, one granddaughter, through God, has blessed me with a great-grandchild.

Though I mention just a few of God's blessings on me, I know it would take a very large book with many, many pages to list all the wondrous blessings God has placed upon me. The largest and best, His Son and my Savior Jesus Christ. As I turned my face toward Jesus, my life began to change. Through Jesus, my thoughts turned from myself to God and helping my fellow man.

As I moved along on my journey with Jesus, messages began to turn over and over in my mind. The feelings were overwhelming for me to write these messages down in poems.

It is my prayer that whoever reads these messaged poems will read them in the spirit that they were written. These poems could have been written by you, about you, and for you. Perhaps you will see moments and circumstances where the message might have come directly from your heart. I pray that if in some way you feel these messages are written with you in mind, that it lifts your eyes and heart to Father God. I pray that any message you accept as fitting into your life will bring you closer to our Father God. In some way, you may be brought into a closer loving relationship with God. Through that, His great loving glory will fill you with unspeakable joy.

The Holy Spirit places the idea and then the words to be written in my hand to put forth a message.

I prayerfully hope that as you read these poems, you will enjoy and accept any message that may touch your heart.

Remember, God's blessings are always there in the love He has for you, and when things may get you down, hold out your hand, for the Father is there to take your hand and draw you to Him and the safety of His wonderful Love.

God bless all and enjoy!

Gerald M. Allen

Welcome Home

When you're tired and you're weary
And you wonder where you're at
When your days are dark and dreary
And you can't help looking back.

To the days that are of sorrow
Of the sins and wrongs you did
And you worry of tomorrow
For you know that they're not hid.

There's a different way to do this
There's a path that leads to bliss
To a Man that walked among us
And He'll greet you with a kiss.

He took our sins upon Him
As they nailed Him to a cross
And through his blood and suffering
He died but was not lost.

For in the ground three days He lay
For all our sins to pay
The Lord our God then raised Him up
From the ground in which he lay.

So trust in Him, believe in Him
He'll lead you on your way
And through his blood and suffering
He will wash your sins away.

He will come to you and live in you
And guide you night and day
So praise our God who sent his Son
Our sins for Him to pay.

So never look behind you
But keep your eye ahead
For Christ our Lord, the King of Kings
Has risen from the dead.

And on the day you kneel to Him
That sits upon His throne
He'll take your hand and lift you up
And tell you, Welcome Home.

Praise to Jesus

From the moment that I wake up
To the day that lies ahead
For my Holy God in Heaven
I do get me out of bed.

And the day that is before me
Let me walk it in God's way
For the path that God does show me
Is a place for me to pray.

As I raise my hands to reach to Him
And praise His Holy name
He holds me close and comforts me
That reaches deep within.

And when I sin
And sometimes go astray
He holds me up and strengthens me
And He loves me anyway.

Oh, Lord my God, do make of me
Of that which is Your will
To live my life with faithfulness
For His cross that's on that hill.

My heart, my soul, my spirit too
I gladly give to Him
He gave His life and spilled His blood
To wash away my sins.

And on the day I kneel to Him
Before His mighty throne
He'll take my hand and say to me
My child, you're welcome home.

A New Path

I was on a lonely path
There was darkness in my past
And I felt the darkness
Closing in on me.

Then I raised my hands above
And prayed, God, I need Your love
For I felt the time
Was running out on me.

But He wanted me to see
First things need there to be
Then a man of God
I went therefore to see.

Said the man of God to me
Of a thing that had to be
Then with the water and the Word
He baptized me.

I confessed of all my sins
And sweet Jesus took them in
And He nailed them to
A cross on Calvary.

When Christ washed away my sins
Jesus took his place within
With a blinding love
That took a hold of me.

Now I'm on a Godly path
And there's brightness
Here at last, and I feel
His awesome love surrounding me.

Now I raise my hands above
And I thank Him for His love
And forever more
I'll pray My God to Thee.

The Spirit

On the pillow lay my head
Of sweet dreams I had in bed
When the Holy Spirit
Did awaken me.

Hey you raise your weary head
And then get you out of bed
For there are some things
I want to say to Thee.

Let's go into the den
And there grab a pad and pen
And you better bring some
Coffee on your way.

For if it takes all night
We're gonna get this right
So you write down
All the things I have to say.

Now He talked to me all night
Of the things for me to write
And He didn't stop
Until the break of day.

Now you wonder what he said?

Well some night when you're in bed
With your pillow tucked
Beneath your sleepy head.

And the Spirit He will come
Before your sleep is done
For at that time
He will awaken thee.

And He'll keep you up all night
Of the things for you to write
For there are some things
He'll want to say to thee.

For the words they won't be few
Of the things He'll say to you
So write down of all
He has to say.

To others you will say
How the Spirit had His way
And how He talked to you
All night till break of day.

Then with slightly bended ear
They'll lean close so they may hear
Then they'll look to you and ask

Well what'd He say?

Reflections

When I look into the looking glass
And in there I do see
And I wonder of the image
That is looking back at me.

Is he truthful, is he faithful
Is there anything he's hid
Has he gave a full confession
Of all the things he did?

Does he do what God does ask of him
Does he do it right away
Does he try to live in righteousness
On each and every day?

In Christ His name, I pray for him
To wash away his sins
Yes, it is the answer
To the questions asked of him.

For the image in that looking glass
The image that I see
The image in the looking glass
That's the image there of me.

I pray someday in the looking glass
There the image I will see
Will be the image there of Jesus Christ
And the image not of me.

Old Mother Hubbard

Old Mother Hubbard
Went to her cupboard
But alas
Her poor cupboard was bare.

With a family to feed
How great was her need
For the food
That of which was not there.

Then from our Father above
Came His message of love
Through the Spirit
That all we do share.

Give heed to their need
And follow God's lead
For His children
The burden they bare.

Then to all of God's glory
Make happy this story
And give all
Your best, plus a prayer.

God Bless

How Amazing All This Is

Just look yourself around you
On a very busy day
Of all that does surround you
Our God made for us one day.

The morning as the sun appears
So brightly there above
It's from the Lord our God
To show us all His love.

How bright there is the color
Of the clear blue skies above
It is God's glorious way
That starts our brand new day.

The green, green grass
The flowers and the trees
And what a sweet aroma
That attracts the little bees.

God did bring forth great animals
How different they all be
But in them be a beauty
For all of us to see.

The vastness of the universe
Of all we cannot see
And of the stars at night
How countless they all be.

There is one special thing
Our Father set apart
The children in their laughter
That puts a smile within your heart.

So never take for granted
The things that God has done
As a sacrifice for all of us
He gave his only Son.

Christ our Lord did die for us
So that we may live
Don't close your eyes but look around
Of all that He does give

Now within your heart you know
You know
How amazing all this is!

Empty Vessel Made of Clay

To the day that stands before me
As you guide me on my way
And your hand that does protect me
For Your plan that fits this day.

Without you Lord my Father
I'm a useless wretched man
But in you Lord my God
I always feel I can.

Your awesome great stability
You're ever still the same
Please give me Christ's humility
That I may glorify Your name.

Help me keep and love my neighbors
Give the poor a helping hand
Make me humble to all others
Make of me a useful man.

Oh Lord my God my Father
It's to You that I do pray
For Lord my God without You
I'm an empty vessel made of clay.

So take this empty vessel
That's only made of clay
And put there God within it
Of Your will, and only of Your way.

Get Out of that Ditch

Now you've driven down life's highway
And you run off in the ditch
So think of all the different ways
In your life that you can switch.

In your mind look deep within your heart
Feel the need there of the poor
Or is it there within your heart
To those you will ignore?

The need there for your fellow man
Is a need to not ignore
For when you help and see you can
You'll want to do much more.

The thought of yours for others
Fills the Spirit full of joy
From the Lord our God, through Jesus Christ
God's own begotten boy.

In Jesus Christ, devote your life
In the ditch you'll be no more
For all our sins Christ gave his life
And opened us a door.

As the Lord our God does change you
To the life that Jesus gives
Christ our Lord His life he give
And He did so we may live.

Now your back upon life's highway
Keep your eyes there straight ahead
Thank Christ our Lord and Savior
Whom our God raised from the dead.

So ask the Holy Spirit
How be the best that you can give
And praise our God in heaven
For He is the God that lives.

I Wonder

Sometimes I sit and wonder
Of Heaven which is my Father's home
He'll show to us His wonders
From there we'll never roam.

I'll be there with my wife again
Father called her home to be with Him
We'll remember years of married life
Fifty-two years, a gift to us from Him.

My mom, my dad, my family
I pray there all they be
And there my grandmas and my grandpas
But how can all this be?

For the last that I did see them
They were much older then than me
But now they're up in Heaven
The same age we seem to be.

Our God will tell to us great stories
Of Jesus Christ His son
How through his blood and suffering
The victory for all of us He won.

Our God will bid us move along
And we will hear our Father say
I love you all, My children
Now run along and play.

Happy Birthday, Jesus

T'was the night we call Christmas
When here upon earth
A Virgin called Mary
To our Savior gave birth.

He was born in a manger
His bed made of hay
A great shining star
Shone on the place where he lay.

The Angels told shepherds
Of this new baby boy
They came there to worship
For he filled them with joy.

Three wise men they followed
The star from above
And set there their gifts
And worshiped in love.

On this cold winter night
Father sent us the One
To give us great light
Lord Jesus His Son.

So let us exclaim
To our Father above
With the birth of our Savior
You've shown us Your love.

With all of this said
As we go off to bed
Merry Christmas to All
Through Jesus Christ are we led.

A Letter to Mary

Hello, Mary, you don't know me
But I know your Holy name
How an Angel came before you
And did call your Holy name.

To give a message from the Father
You are the Blessed chosen one
To receive and then to carry
Jesus Christ the Father's Son.

When the test was put to Joseph
How He heard the Angel say
The child is of our Father
So wed thee then to Mary, for it is to be God's way.

Our God the Holy Father
To Bethlehem, He led you there
He placed a star above You
So all would know his Son was there.

You there became the mother
Of Jesus Christ, God's only Son
You're a mother like no other
Our Savior's life was there begun.

Through our Heavenly dear Father
We bless your Holy name
With the birth of our dear Savior
The world will never be the same.

As the Mother of our Savior
From our Father up above
Makes the day we all call Christmas
A Holy Day that's filled with love.

So a very Merry Christmas
To each and every one
For from Lord our God the Father
Came to us Jesus Christ His Holy Son.

So thank you, sweet, sweet Mary
That our Father did favor you
With the birth of Christ our Savior
We can become brand-new.

Humility

Humility, Humility
What an easy word to say
Through Jesus Christ our Savior
His humility shows to us His way.

As you wake up every morning
God's great love for you within
Upon your knees show honor
Humble all yourself to Him.

Then through your day with others
And one may vex you on your way
Be humble and forgiving
A prayer for him do say.

Be ever oh so careful
Of a thing within called pride
Within your flesh it tries so hard
To put humility on the side.

Our pride will only lead us
To a path that's very wide
It reaches down within our souls
Our humility there to hide.

When pride does rule upon our lives
It becomes a raging sin
For then we live to praise ourselves
When all our praise belongs to Him.

So every day upon your knees
To the Lord our God do pray
Please, Lord, do keep me humble
That I may follow in Christ's way.

Take pleasure in your weakness
In Christ, He'll make you strong
It humbles us our weakness
In Jesus Christ we now belong.

When the Lord our God removes from us
Our pride which is our sin
We then can die unto ourselves
So God can wholly move within.

When you know that you are nothing
And Lord God is all in all
It's then God will exalt you
For you harkened to His call.

When humbled then to God and man
And empty there inside
Our Holy God then lives in you
Leaving pride no place to hide.

Our Dearest Friend

God created in His image
A life that is in you and me
A special person that is you
A special person that is me.

He molded oh so carefully
Our lives he had in mind
For every life be different
And all a special kind.

With this life God gave to us
In this life what should we do
Should we only care then for ourselves
Or should we love and care for you.

Our lives through love is meant to share
With all our fellow man
To help the needy and the poor
In every way we can.

It is good to love your neighbor
To your foe love him the same
Be loving and forgiving
Do it all in Jesus' name.

When Christ sat on that mountainside
And the sermon He did give
His words were meant for all of us
His guide how we should live.

And there within God's Holy Book
His Holy words for us to see
He speaks there in to all of us
Of a better life from Him to be.

This special creature God made of us
With a special plan for us to be
Lord Jesus Christ did spill his blood
From sin to set us free.

Let God then make the person
The one He wants for us to be
The plan He made before our birth
With great love for you and me.

Pray to God the Father
Through Jesus Christ his Son
Worthy is the Lord our God
For He is the true and Holy One.

In fellowship do praise his Holy name
All your love to Him do send
For the Lord our God in heaven
Wants to be our dearest friend.

Teach and Serve

Lord God Almighty Father
Sent Jesus Christ His only son
Humbly He came to serve
Our Savior Christ, God's chosen one.

Christ with great humility
Does show how we should live
Our fellow man for us to serve
Our love to them we give.

A humble life did Jesus live
Loving Grace He freely gives
His loving arms He opens them
To believe and come to Him.

Humbled unto God and man
In God's love He has a plan
He lived a life that had no sin
He teaches us to be like Him.

His precious blood upon the cross
To wash away our sins
We died to sin upon His cross
Now Jesus Christ He lives within.

Praise God our Holy Father
Praise Jesus Christ His only son
Spirit lead us in this Trinity
Our newborn life through Christ He won.

In Christ My Love

Oh, Holy Lord, oh, Jesus Christ
It is of You, that is our Light
Your loving heart, such tenderness
Your gracious love, does give us rest.

Your loving arms, You open wide
When trouble comes, we hide inside
You hold us up, and wipe our tears
Your awesome love, relieves our fears.

Oh, what a joy, to know the One
My Savior Christ, who is God's Son
Upon the cross, is where He died
God raised Him up, unto His side.

Oh, Jesus Christ, He lives again
He comes to us, and lives within
Through Christ His blood, and suffering
He washes us, of all our sin.

Through Jesus Christ, I humbly kneel
To serve my God, and fellow man
Your will, my God, do show to me
It is Your love, that set me free.

I pray in Christ, I may be found
When here on earth, that trumpet sounds
Dear Lord my God, to you I pray
In Christ I'll be, on judgment day.

Rolled Away

Jesus Christ His life He give
And He did so we may live
When they led Him with His cross to Calvary.

They raised Him on that cross
For they thought that He had lost
But 'twas on that hill
My Savior died for me.

In the tomb where Jesus lay
All our sins for Him to pay
A giant stone was rolled
To close my Savior in.

Three days within He lay
For our sins He there did pay
When God's mighty hand
He rolled that stone away.

He rolled away, He rolled away
With His mighty hand
God rolled that stone away.

God spoke to Him inside
And said, My Son, arise
For today's the day
That stone is rolled away.

God called Him, come outside
Son, You'll soon be at my side
Resurrected!
Forever you will live.

Now with Christ at God's right hand
The Holy Spirit is in man
Thank you, Lord my God
Who rolled that stone away.

He rolled away, He rolled away
With the Father's love
He rolled that stone away.

God praise Your Holy Name
The world will never be the same
With Your loving hand
You rolled that stone away.

Jesus died upon that Cross
But there he was not lost
For belief in Him
God rolls our sins away.

Confess of all your sins
And you'll die to live again
Through Jesus Christ our Lord
God rolls our sins away.

Look Up

Look up, unto the heavens
To our Father up above
Look up, to our Lord Jesus Christ
Whom our Father sent with love.

Look up, to God's great chosen one
His own begotten Son
With humbleness He came to serve
Our Father's only Son.

Look up, to Him upon that cross
Jesus Christ his blood did spill
With nails they did pierce His skin
For It was the Father's will.

Look up, to our Lord Jesus Christ
New life the Father give
Trust in Him, believe in Him
And there be born again.

Look up, to keep your eyes on Christ
Let Him lead you from within
Let His Holiness consume your soul
That you may live to love like Him.

Look up, to Christ our Savior
Through Him and Him alone
Jesus Christ the only way
To the Father on His throne.

Look up, unto Jesus Christ
As He sets at God's right hand
Look up, for Christ He lives again
And for us He lives within.

Lord God My Everything

How big are you, oh, Lord, my God,
How little here am I?
I often set and wonder
As I gaze up in the sky.

How amazing is the sky so blue
As I set and think of you
For every day you give me, Lord
It's a day that is brand-new.

Are you in that cloud up there
Or the one that's over there?
The Lord my God's in both of them
My God is everywhere.

The works of you, Almighty God
Some things we cannot see
The things we see we know not how
All these wondrous things can be.

Lord my life belongs to You
To sin I died upon Christ's cross
And now with newborn life
In Christ I live to You.

Thank you, oh, Lord my God
All the things for me You do
I thank You, Lord, to the end of time
Just to show my love for You.

All that is this universe
Everything God comes from You
From the biggest to the smallest
Oh, God, it all belongs to You.

You keep in perfect order
All the wondrous things You do
Through each and every second
With great love that comes from You.

Without you, Lord
No air to breathe, no beating of my heart
But oh so many blessings
Came from the very start.

The hair once red upon my head
Now gray it has become
I thank You, God, for all those years
All my blessings from You have come.

When it be Your will, Lord my God
My life on earth is through
I pray, dear God, You take my soul
To be eternally there with You.

God First

As I wake up every morning
A fresh day that is all new
The first thing that I think of
God I will start my day with You.

With the Spirit here within me
In Your word I start my day
Give me knowledge and great wisdom
That will lead me in Christ's way.

Let my heart be oh so tender
Let my words be sweet and true
Let the Spirit that's within me
Show the love that comes from You.

And as my day does move along
In Your word do keep me strong
In loving and forgiving
Lord keep me from all wrong.

Let me be a blessing
To all my fellow man
Let me help them in their needs
In every way I can.

As this day You gave to me
Let me close it in Your word
I pray dear Lord if the morning comes
We will do it all again.

Always There

As I reach out with my fingers
And stretch them out to touch the air
The air I cannot feel
But, Father God, I now You're there.

With every beat within my heart
I know they all do come from You
You were there before my start
With a plan that is all new.

Though I be unable
To see the Glory of Your face
With the tenderness You placed in me
You rule my life with all Your Grace.

Through Your Son Lord Jesus Christ
With His blood my sins washed clean
He came here then to live in me
And I, to live through Him.

The truth that is in all Your words
Your truth has set me free
From my mouth the words I say
I pray come from You and not from me.

Through you, sweet Lord Jesus
I praise the Father's Holy name
Within Your arms, Lord Jesus
You have released me from all shame.

On my knees I worship You
Your name the highest of the high
Dear Lord my God, do hold me up
For God in You I'll never die.

Cleansing Blood

What a Great Arising
Has come upon my soul
My Savior Christ forgave me
Without the need of gold.

The silver in this world
It has no hold on me
For the only thing that's precious
Is His blood that cleanses me.

The awesome love of Jesus
Is here within my heart
Since my life I give to Jesus
We never more will part.

The Holy Word in Jesus
God sent the Word for me
To give His life upon the cross
Christ gave his life for me.

Through the Holy Blood of Jesus
His blood it cleanses me
The sweet, sweet name of Jesus
The Word came to set me free.

So Thank You, Sweet Lord Jesus
Your life to rescue me
With the blood You spilled upon that cross
That precious blood it cleanses me.

Within Your Arms, Lord Jesus
May You ever hold me there
For in Your Arms, Lord Jesus
There I live without despair.

I love you, sweet, sweet Jesus
Through Your light I now can see
Your blood You spilled upon that cross
That blood it cleanses me.

Temptation

As you move along from day-to-day
With the Love of Christ within
As you try to live a way
A life that's free of sin.

But there from out of nowhere
In Your flesh this thing moves in
It's an ugly thing, temptation
That wants to lead you onto sin.

It tugs and pulls and twists you
Tries it's best to fill your mind
This ugly thing, temptation
As it sneaks up from behind.

You try your best to fight it
Doing all the best you can
This ugly thing, temptation
Sometimes gets the upper hand.

You know the day will come
Temptation comes again
You'll fight it off with all your might
But you see temptation win.

Don't ever get discouraged
And think you just can't win
Go to our Lord Jesus
Who will keep you from all sin.

When temptation comes upon you
Jesus Christ can lead your way
That ugly thing, temptation
Will not win here on this day

Upon your knees to Father God
Give temptation when it comes
He will fight this fight
And sin he'll keep you from.

We try to fight temptation
With our flesh how weak we be
Make God your only all in all
From temptation then be free.

Open Up Your Door

Are you in a place in life
You don't really want to be
Are you locked behind a door
That just won't set you free?

Are there things behind that door
Are they sins and wrongs you did
Are they kept behind that door
For there you think they're hid?

Has the burden there behind that door
Ruled your life from day to day
Do you hope for there to be a way
To wash those sins away?

There is a way to do it
There is a man that holds the key
To open up and cleanse the sins
That has kept you locked within.

The sins locked behind that door
Ask Jesus to forgive
Jesus will unlock that door
And wash all sins within.

Behind that door that Jesus cleaned
And washed away the sins
He will take the key and lock that door
That you need never go in again.

And if a sin you do commit
The sin please hide no more
Ask Jesus Christ to forgive
And to Heaven open up your door.

He Comforts Me

When trials are before me
And my way I cannot see
In Jesus' arms he holds me
With His love He comforts me.

When my heart is filled with sorrow
And my soul does trouble me
With a burden on my shoulders
My Lord Jesus comforts me.

He relieves me of my sorrow
With His Love He touches me
From the things that once were sorrow
Jesus Christ has set me free.

Oh what joy there is in Jesus
To my joy He lives in me
I worship you Lord Jesus
Your great Love You give to me.

The things that stand before me
No matter what they be
All my trust I give you Jesus
For you died to rescue me.

Your Plan

When Father God created you
He had certain things in mind
With all His Love He made of you
A very special kind.

He put there deep within you
His Love how great a gift
Great tenderness within your heart
To give your soul a lift.

And if somehow you've gone astray
Your way you can't find back
Fix your eyes on our Lord Jesus
And those stripes upon his back.

For us Christ took those stripes
Gave his blood upon that Cross
A ransom He there did pay
So we would not be lost.

Put your trust in our Lord Jesus
Walk His path with Christ each day
Keep your eyes upon His actions
On your knees to Him do pray.

Now your back again with Jesus
And God's plan He has for you
Just over that horizon
Where the skies are bright and blue.

Just over that horizon
It's not that far away
It's only just a little hill
If you follow in Christ's way.

Obey His Word and do His will
That you may understand
Jesus stands before you
With God's plan there in His hand.

Go There Every Day

Here's a little thought
That may help you start your day
On your knees to pray to Jesus
Have you been there yet today?

Do you read the words of Jesus
His Love for you is strong
If you spend your day with Jesus
He will keep you from all wrong

In His words there is great wisdom
It is His word that shows the way
Be humble unto Jesus
Put your trust in Him today.

Give thanks to our Lord Jesus
Who gave His Life upon the Cross
His stripes, his blood and suffering
So we would not be lost.

Now then every morning
Before your feet do reach the floor
Pray on your knees to Jesus
That he may open Heaven's door.

Little Bits of Heaven

There are little bits of Heaven
Our Father sends to us each day
They're little things called children
So very precious in their way.

From the time of their conception
To the moment of their birth
They are from God our Father
Who sent them here to earth.

With great joy these tiny babies
God lays them in our arms
His wondrous love that's in us
To protect them from all harm.

Those tiny little faces
Those tiny little cries
You know the Love of God
Lay right before your eyes.

We know these little children
Rely on us each day
They look to us for guidance
And to love them every day.

With love do keep your children
And raise them in God's Word
Teach them of Lord Jesus
For he is the Father's Word.

Look upon our children
There's great lessons there within
Jesus said to be with Him
We must first be just like them.

Little children in us they trust
The lessons there to see
For as our children trust in us
Our trust in God must be.

We are of God our Father
Through Jesus Christ the Chosen One
We are His little children
As is, Jesus Christ His Son.

We must be as the little child
Seek the Father through His Son
In Father God we're not alone
But someday at His throne.

Our Light

Our Father God in Heaven
On this earth as you look down,
Guide us on your narrow path
In this Newborn Life we found.

It is through your Son Jesus Christ
Our Savior from above,
It is His Blood that cleanses us
With everlasting love.

Your awesome love through Jesus
His Life He lived sin free,
As men we are all sinners
But Jesus gives us light to see.

Every day we roam this earth
Your hands in all we live,
Without you, Lord, there is no life
It's from You our life You give.

We thank You for Your Holy Word
In Your Word we all should live,
And when we sometimes sin,
Your love You still do give.

Lead us, Lord, to where there is no night
Through your Son that lights our way,
On our knees to You, dear God,
Forevermore we pray.

Awaken Me

As I read Your Word, oh Lord my God
The great truth how sweet it be,
It is the truth God's Holy Word
Came to earth to set me free.

Lead me, Lord, this sinful man
In Your Word, God, make me strong,
To obey Your each and all commands
And, Father, keep me from all wrong.

Through You, oh God my Father
Your Son who ransomed me,
In me the Holy Spirit
With Your Word that does guide me.

You placed me here upon this earth
With a plan for me to be,
Father, may it be your will
Your plan fulfilled in me.

Great praise and all the Glory
I bring it to Your throne,
Upon my knees show honor
For You left me not alone.

Awaken me my soul, oh Lord
Hold me in Your loving hands,
That I may see the face
Never seen before by man.

Just a Limb

I pray dear God
And praise Your Holy Name,
With all the love within me
Let me Glorify Your Name.

From day to day through Jesus
Your love You show to me,
Through the Word Your Son Lord Jesus
Who died to rescue me.

To give Your only Son Lord Jesus
Whom man nailed upon that Cross,
With his Blood He cleansed our sins
With his Life He paid the cost.

You sacrificed Your only Son
So we could live again,
Then with love You sent your Spirit
To guide us from within.

Thank you God my Father
For all the blessings placed on me,
Jesus Christ is the root
And I but a limb upon his tree.

Little Child of God

He who died upon the Cross
To save a wretch like me,
Upon my knees I pray to him
To clear my eyes that I may see.

I confessed to Him of all my sins
With His Blood He washed them clean,
I died to sin upon His Cross
Jesus Christ now lives within.

Now my Lord and Savior
He walks with me each day,
He holds my hand and guides me
As he moves me to His way.

His wondrous love surrounds me
He fills my heart so full of joy,
In my life great things he does
To God I'm just His little boy.

To be a little child of God
There is no better thing to be,
Great everlasting love from Him
His Son's light so I may see.

Oh what love I have for Him
My Father God the Holy One,
Someday I pray to see His face
When my life on earth is done.

I pray that I will be with Him
To kneel before His throne,
Forever more I'll praise His Name
My God, my God alone.

Your Day with Jesus

When you wake up every morning
You know not what lies ahead,
Roll out upon your knees
There right beside your bed.

Thank Jesus for His sacrifice
His Life He gave for you,
His crimson Blood upon that Cross
So live this day brand-new.

Ask Him for forgiveness
To Jesus Christ do pray,
For guidance from the Spirit
As He leads you on your way.

Jesus takes your griefs and sins
So enjoy the life He gives,
Glorify and praise His Name
For the life you have is His.

Throughout your day with others
Keep Jesus on your mind,
As you spend your day with Jesus
You'll be gentle and so kind.

With this day Jesus gave to you
Look to your fellow man,
See if there be a way
To help them if you can.

The Lord your God His eye on you
On each and every day,
To help you not to go astray
But have your walk with Jesus every day.

Show all your love for Jesus
Keep it strong within your heart,
Keep it ever present in your mind
From Jesus then you'll never part.

You woke with Him this morning
Before you go to bed and turn off the light,
On your knees do pray to Jesus
That He keep you through the night.

And if it be His will
Jesus calls you to come home,
Upon your knees show honor
As you kneel there at His throne.

Jesus Saved Me

I woke up this morning
To start a new day,
On my knees to Lord Jesus
To show me the way.

I know my Lord Jesus
We talk every day,
His love that surrounds me
To show me the way.

His words how they comfort
They reach deep within,
His words I do follow
To keep me from sin.

I no longer need
Worldly things I can see,
My life is to Jesus
He lives now in me.

Oh lead me Lord Jesus
Your Spirit in me,
Your hand ever gentle
Your love to guide me.

You saved me from sin
When You died on that cross,
A newborn I live
I'm no longer lost.

If you want Jesus
In your life every day,
Confess on your knees
He'll show you the way.

He'll hold you, He loves you
His love never dies,
He'll call you someday
To His home in the sky.

Through you my Lord Jesus
The Father I'll see,
I love you Lord Jesus
On that Cross you saved me.

God Time

Do you turn your thoughts to Jesus
As you wake up there in bed?
Do you thank our God the Father
Who raised Him from the dead?

Do you take the time to spend with God
In His Holy Book to start your day?
Do you take the time to read the Words
To help guide you in His way?

Do you feel that you don't have the time
To spend with God on every day?
Remember without You God
There would be no brand-new day.

What is most important
In your day that lay ahead?
Should not it be your God
Before you're out of bed?

Place your hand upon your chest
Feel the beating of your heart,
Father God controlled that beat
Right from the very start.

How Father God does love you
You're always on his mind,
He's with you every second
God never falls behind.

Father God makes time for you
Every second, every minute, every hour, every day,
Never does He leave you
He's there and there to stay.

So see if there may be a way
To arrange your time each day,
To spend more time with your God
On your knees to Him do pray.

The precious time you spend with God
In His heart he holds you near,
And if you have a burden
He relieves you of all fear.

The Father is your God
So take the time to be with Him,
Be humble unto your God
Show the love you have for Him.

The things that are of this world
They are things that go away,
But if you give your love to God
For eternity you'll be with God to stay.

If these verses seem quite lengthy
Father wants for me to say,
With all His heart He loves you
And He wants time with you each day.

Trinity

As I wake up each morning
My first thought it be,
God the Father, God the Son
And God the Spirit in me.

I pray on my knees
To God's Trinity,
God the Father, God the Son
And God the Spirit in me.

Thank you sweet Jesus
For your light that I see,
God the Father, God the Son,
And God the Spirit in me.

With Jesus my Lord
On His path where He leads,
To God the Father, God the Son,
And God the Spirit in me.

I turn neither left, nor to the right
But eyes straight ahead,
To God the Father, God the Son,
And God the Spirit in me.

God's Holy Word, has set me free
My life I live new to God's Trinity,
God the Father, God the Son,
And God's Holy Spirit in me.

Then and Now

When I was down, sorrow within me.
When I was down, Jesus knew all my fears.
When I was down, trials before me.
When I was down, Jesus felt all my tears.

When I was down, on my knees there before Him
When I was down, confessed all my sins.
When I was down, I asked His forgiveness
When I was down, He forgave me my sins.

When I was down, His hand reaching to me.
When I was down, hugged my hand into His.
When I was down, He raised me up gently.
When I was down, His arms drew me in.

Now I am His, He walks here beside me.
Now I am His, He shows me His way.
Now I am His, it's His Word I follow.
Now I am His, on my knees Lord I Pray.

Now I am His, wherever He leads me.
Now I am His, go wherever I may.
Now I am His, great joy that's within me.
Now I am His, what a great joyous day.

Now I am His, both now and forever.
Now I am His, Sing Praise to His Name.
Now I am His, Grace He has given.
When God calls me home, I'll be there with him.

The Glory Road

I was on a path, a lonely path
As dark as it could be,
So many sins there in my past
That had ahold on me.

I stumbled down that lonely path
So dark I could not see,
And there in all that darkness
I fell upon my knees.

I raised my eyes to heaven
A light then came to me,
The light it was Lord Jesus
To light the path for me.

He took my hand, He picked me up
I told Him of my sins,
I asked Him for forgiveness
He cleansed the sins within.

I'm on the Glory Road to heaven
To the Father and the King,
They're both there up in heaven
And it is to them I sing.

I'll sing Your praise and follow You
No matter where You lead,
I'm on the Glory Road to heaven
To the Father and the King.

Where there was great darkness
A light now shines within,
On the Glory Road to heaven
To the Father and the King.

The Father's joy does fill my soul
It's in that joy I sing,
On the Glory Road to heaven
To the Father and the King.

With Jesus Christ I'll walk that road
Up to those Pearly Gates,
On the Glory Road to heaven
To the Father and the King.

On the Glory Road to heaven
Christ walks with me each day,
On the Glory Road, there at the end
Father calls me home to stay.

I'll be in all God's Glory
Evermore to be with Him,
On the Glory Road to heaven
Father God will take me in.

Who

Who raises the sun
Shows stars through the night?
Who holds up the moon
Till dawn's early light?

Who opens your eyes
As you lay there in bed?
Who is it that guides
Your day just ahead?

Who is it that makes
The clouds up above?
Who is it that gives
A life filled with love?

Who is it that sends
Rain from the sky?
Who waters the trees
That grow oh so high?

Who is it that knows
Every hair on your head?
Who is it that knows
Every word that you said?

Who is it that knows
Every thought in your mind?
Who is it that knows
When you're not being kind?

Who is it that gives
His light unto you?
Who is it that has
Your plan that is new?

Who is it that does
These things every day?
Who gives us His word
To lead us His way?

His name you don't know?
I'll give you a clue,
It's Father our God
Who forever loves you.

My Love, My Wife, My Ronnie

When we were yet but children
It was so long ago,
But things here in my memory
Seems like a day ago.

I see her in her beauty
I feel her warm and tender heart,
Oh what great love I had for her
Right from the very start.

In marriage Father bound us
Both together in His Name,
I eighteen and her sixteen
Two Together as one we soon became.

With love God gave to us
Four daughters one by one,
And everything within us
Was our love for everyone.

A loving wife my Ronnie
Four daughters gave to me,
A special sparkle in her eyes
Clear for all to see.

When trials came upon us
And we thought our love won't last,
With God's loving hands upon us
He put those trials there in our past.

Our lifetime spent together
Our love through years did grow,
The things that I remember
Was not that long ago.

Fifty-two years of marriage
With Ronnie as my wife,
My Love, My Wife, My Ronnie
And yes, she was my life.

God gave us all these many years
His blessings day by day,
Father God then called her home
Now she's there with Him to stay.

It's been four years since she had to go
Each day seems like a year,
In joy she's there with Father God
But in my eye there's still a tear.

I LOVE YOU! AND MISS YOU!

Blood of Love

Jesus came from Father
On a cold December night,
The only Child of our God
To bring the world His light.

God's only Son, Lord Jesus
Father's Word was born a man,
To teach us and to guide us
To love our God and fellow man.

As a boy God's Son, Lord Jesus
Set about to fill the Father's plan,
His wisdom has no boundaries
To fulfill our God's command.

Baptized in the Jordan
God's Lamb, God's only Son,
With the dove of Peace upon Him
John knew He was the one to come.

Tempted by the devil
No match for Christ was he,
Said Satan, get behind me
God's Word is all I need.

The miracles of Jesus
All could see He was God's Son,
With blinded eyes and covered ears
A plot to kill Him had begun.

Betrayed to them by Judas
Arrested, crucify Him came their call,
Pilot tried to free Him
Free Barabbas shouted all.

Lord Jesus scourged then bore His cross
To that hill called Calvary,
His care not for Himself
But His care to rescue me.

What love was sent from Heaven
From my Father God to me,
To give His one begotten Son
From sin to set me free.

There is love in the blood
Of the Man from Galilee,
Who gave His life upon that cross
And spilled His blood for me.

Lord Jesus and Me

Lord Jesus with me
On my knees as I pray,
Lord Jesus, Lord Jesus,
Lord Jesus and me.

My heart and my soul
Filled with Jesus each day,
Jesus, sweet Jesus,
Please show me Your way.

How tender, how loving,
How forgiving is He,
Jesus, my Jesus,
He lives here in me.

Jesus, Lord Jesus,
He lives here in me,
Lord Jesus my Savior
Lord Jesus and me.

He leads me, He guides me,
His Words bring me to Him,
My Savior, Lord Jesus
He frees me from sin.

Keep me Lord Jesus
In Your arms every day,
Jesus, Lord Jesus,
Through You I do pray.

Jesus, Lord Jesus,
I kneel at Your Cross,
I look up to You
Where You paid the cost.

Your Blood spilled on me
As I kneel at Your Cross,
My sins there washed clean
I'm no longer lost.

With love and forgiveness
Your Light that I see,
Hold my hand, Jesus
To the Father take me.

Angels That Do Fly

Have you ever been in danger,
You see and feel it pass you by,
You're sure you should be injured,
But you're not and know not why.

You look around and wonder
What did keep you from all harm,
You could not see the Angel
That had you held there in his arms.

God knows what lies before you
As you move on through your day,
His Angels fly around you
To protect you on your way.

We know our God has Angels
Sent to watch us while at home,
His Angels fly above us
Wherever we may roam.

So when you feel in danger
And you watch it pass you by,
Know it was God's Angels
For they had you in their eye.

Thank you God my Father
For Your Angels that do fly,
You rose your Son, Lord Jesus
Now through Him we'll never die.

God's Holy flying Angels
They protect not only you,
For it's you and our Lord Jesus
Who forever lives in you.

God's Angels always with us
They are with us to the end,
They take our hand with Jesus
And fly us safely home to Him.

Meet My Friend Lord Jesus

Are you walking down a wayward path
On a path that's filled with sin?
Then let me ask a question
Have you ever turned to Him?

Is it time you meet Lord Jesus
And confess of all your sins?
Is it time you meet Him on His Cross
There to wash away your sins?

On His Cross there with Lord Jesus
Die to all your sins,
You die there with Lord Jesus
But yet be born again.

Lord Jesus lay there in His tomb,
Three days our sins to pay,
Our Father God then raised Him up,
From the tomb in which He lay.

The Newborn Life that Jesus gives
The sins of yours before,
With Jesus' Blood they are washed clean
And God remembers them no more.

At the foot of Lord Jesus' Cross
We all look up to Him,
God's only son Lord Jesus
Died so we could live through Him.

So meet my dear friend Jesus
Read His Words on every day,
The words that are from Jesus
Help and guide you in His way.

Let Jesus take control
Give your trust and life to Him,
Let Jesus make the change
That you be more and more like Him.

So love your God, for God loves you
He always has and always will,
He gave his Son upon that Cross
There high upon that hill.

The sacrifice Lord Jesus made
To bring sinners to repent,
That they be born again
Through the One the Father sent.

Thanks Be to God

To give you thanks oh Lord my God
The words I know seem like so few,
Your wondrous love you faithfulness
New words of thanks I seek for you.

God let the thoughts that fill my mind
Be guided that it's you I find,
Let my lips praise your fame
And my heart shout glory to your name.

On bended knees I bow my head
As the sinner that you know I am,
There I ask you to forgive
You then reach out and take my hand.

You sent your Son to take my sin
To save my soul and live within,
I give you thanks you're always there
Your Spirit lives in me to share.

When morning comes you brightly shine
For I am yours and you are mine,
All through the day your blessings come
I thank you God Great Holy One.

When day is done and night draws near
With you my God there is no fear,
Your loving arms within I sleep
In you my God I rest in peace.

I thank you God with all words I know
I know you're there wherever I go,
My God My God please hold me near
And whisper softly in my ear.

Christmas Is!

How precious is the day
Father sent his Son for me,
Father's one begotten Son
His living gift to set me free.

A baby boy lay in the hay
His mother Mary at his side,
A bright new star in Heaven
Father's sign to where he lie.

Angels brought forth joyous news
To herding shepherds with their sheep,
A Savior born into this world
In Bethlehem is where he sleeps.

They came and worshiped on their knees
To the child there in the hay,
Our Savior and the Prince of Peace
To you dear Lord we pray.

A star above led three wise men there
With gifts to lay at the newborn feet,
The miracle of this Virgin birth
A Newborn Savior there to meet.

Born there on that wintry night
From Father God above,
His name God gave was Jesus
Sent to you and me with love.

He came for our salvation
To lead and guide us in his way,
Tis Christ our dear Lord Jesus
He that glorifies our Christmas day.

Worship Invitation

Please take this invitation
From Father God to you,
Come celebrate our Savior's birth
Who came to rescue you.

Come worship in the Father's House
The Babe born on Christmas Day,
On your knees sing praise to him
As he lay there in the hay.

He came for our salvation
To heal and forgive us of our sins,
He spilled his Blood and gave his Life
So we could live again through him.

This very special birthday
Jesus Christ God's Holy Son,
The Prince of Peace the King of Kings
In Jesus Christ new life through him we won.

Give praise and all the Glory
To the Father God above,
We come to him through Jesus Christ
Sent from God to show his pure sweet love.

Happy Birthday, dear Lord Jesus
What a Glorious Joyous day,
Thank you dear Lord Jesus
It's to you on my knees I pray.

Gift

Though we all be born as sinners
It's not God's plan we stay that way,
The word that He anointed
His commands we should obey.

With this day a gift from God
He knows what this day will bring,
His Holy Spirit guiding us
To God's plan for everything.

His gentle touch upon our hearts
To make us tender and to care,
His Holy Spirit lives within
A Shining Light for all to share.

Though we all be born as sinners
God calls us back to Him,
Through Jesus Christ our Savior
God takes away our sin.

Buried sins in waters deep
God remembers them no more,
Lord Jesus' Blood removes our sin
That we may live forevermore.

A Beautiful World

A beautiful world, thou has made oh my God,
What a beautiful world that I see.
How beautiful the fields of green grass,
And majestic your forests of trees

Oceans of waters all teeming with life
With color amazingly blue,
Great mountains reach high in the sky
Are wonderfully made, God by You.

Animals, God, you placed here upon earth,
What beauty in them we behold,
Your plan ever present in them, Lord my God
In the young and those that are old.

What beauty we see as we gaze up above
To your birds that soar through the air,
Wings that carry them up oh so high
And they glide as they have not a care.

Your presence, oh God, we see everywhere
This great beauty You made for us all,
Father, please take hold of our hand
Hold us up that we may never fall.

All these wonderful things upon earth
All amazing great things that we see,
How joyous my heart, my Lord, I can't wait
To see how beautiful, God thy Heaven will be.

He's

He's the stars that shine in darkness
He's the moon that lights our night,
He's the King my Lord Jesus
He's awesome in His might.

He's the sunrise in the morning
He's my light throughout the day,
He's my knight in shining armor
He's the word that shows my way.

He's the freshness of a springtime rain
He's the warmth of a summer day,
He's the playmate of our children
As He leads them in their play.

He's the beauty all around us
In the grass and in the trees,
He's the beauty of the flowers
That feed His little bees.

He's great in awesome Glory
In autumn shows to me,
He's the multitude of colors
He displays upon His trees.

He's the crispness of a winter day
He's the pure white driven snow,
He's the tender love within us
That protects us from the cold.

He's the one my faith in Him
I pray grows on every day,
He's the tender voice within me
To help me not to go astray.

He's my salvation, my redeemer
He's the keeper of my soul,
Lord Jesus always with me
Where ever I may go.

He's the hand that reaches down to me
He's the hand that holds me up,
He's the bread of life within me
It's His blood that fills my cup.

How many things is Christ to me
I cannot name them all,
When I need a faithful hand
He's Jesus Christ my all in all.

Friends

Let me tell you a story
Of a man named Jesus Christ,
My Savior filled with Glory
Who helps and guides my life.

He teaches me He holds my hand
Through trials that come my way,
He's the King of Kings, the Prince of Peace
He's my friend throughout the day.

How many friends a man may have
There's none that can compare,
To the friendship of Lord Jesus
His love for all to share.

Emanuel God with us
I need his friendship every day,
To teach me in God's Trinity
To hold me on His path along my way.

His friendship in the morning
As I pray beside my bed,
I'm humbled and I'm thankful
Of the day He plans ahead.

He leads me to things unknown
In His Word He makes things clear,
He opens up my eyes to see
And touch my ears that I may hear.

The love that comes from His heart
He places all that love in mine,
His smiling eyes, His shining face
My dearest friend that is so kind.

Oh how great to know Lord Jesus
To me my dearest friend,
He knew me as a sinner
He leads me now his newborn friend.

Instructions

Have you ever bought an object
Very complex in design,
It has to be constructed
With many pieces there to find.

You look around and see a piece
A part that must be used,
You pick it up and wonder
What do I attach this to.

When you try to fit all pieces
To make the object that you want,
You find out very quickly
You can't find the piece you hunt.

As you struggle in your mind
And say these pieces are not right,
You see a book instructions
To make things clearer in your sight.

You pick it up and read the book
It shows how the pieces go,
The pieces come together
Just like the book does show.

You have a life God gave to you
Very complex in design,
A life to be constructed
The one the Father had in mind.

You try to live your life
And things don't fit just right,
Within your mind you struggle
In your flesh you try to fight.

Your mind it leads you here
Then leads you over there,
You just can't fit the pieces
That will lead you anywhere.

Seek the Book of instructions
God's Holy Words to you,
Pick it up and read it
To bring his plan for you in view.

When parts in your life
Are not fitting as they should,
Then read of God's instructions
Things will come together if you would.

God's Book of instructions
Is there for all to share,
All the questions there of life
In God's Holy Book the answers there.

A Day with Jesus

When Jesus comes to waken you
With His gift a day brand-new,
Thank Him for forgiveness
And new life He gives to you.

As you kneel and pray to Him
He who takes away your sins,
Glorify and praise His name
As this day with Him begins.

Take first the time to spend with Him
Read His words learn of His way,
Let the spirit that's within you
Guide your feet throughout the day.

As you move along and wonder
Of all things He leads you to,
Hold them dear within your heart
For these things are meant for you.

He may lead you to a place unknown
To help and bless a fellow man,
And if that be the case
Give help the way you can.

The path He picks this day for you
May be a path that leads to tears,
But know and have faith
He will relieve you of all fears.

He may stop along the way
And bid you rest here for a while,
As you rest and think of Him
Upon your face will come a smile.

For Jesus Christ the Son of God
Is here for all that we may know,
Father God is changing us
That through Jesus Christ our light will glow.

When day is done and night is here
Lord Jesus still remains,
Within our sleep He watches
Till He wakens us again.

Better Way

Start your day with Jesus
For there is no better way,
As you stretch and open up your eyes
Upon your knees then to Him pray.

Throughout the night there as you slept
He was there to give you rest,
His tender loving touch on you
His little child there in His nest.

And now He has bestowed to you
A glorious bright new day,
With all the love He has for you
Upon His path He'll show the way.

So follow Him to where He leads
Ask not the reason why,
Believe and have all trust in Him
As your day with Him goes by.

All things and places He leads you to
Keep them ever in your mind,
For everything He leads you to
Will make you gentle and so kind.

He gave His Blood and Life for you
His love for you so strong,
He died for you upon that Cross
God's Son who did no wrong.

There in the tomb where Jesus lay
Three days to pay the cost,
Father God then raised Lord Jesus
In death He was not lost.

Now He's here he Lives again
Jesus Christ the Father's Son,
Believe and put all trust in Him
In Newborn Life for us He won.

I Believe

I believe in You oh Lord my God
I believe You created all that is,
I believe in Your Son Jesus
Who gave His life that I may live.

I look up to the Heavens
The great vastness filled with stars,
All created by You my Father
Your great love forever ours.

I believe you sent Your Word to earth
To be born here as a man,
I believe He walked on water
I believe in the great I Am.

I believe in all the miracles
Lord Jesus worked through You,
It is because that I believe
I am born again in You.

Problem Solved

If upon this day
You have a problem in your life,
And if you see no answer
To that which caused this strife.

Back off for just a moment
Look to the presence of the Lord,
Ask Him for His guidance
You are the child that He adores.

His love that He pours out to you
Every second of the day,
His hand He reaches out to you
To help and guide you on your way.

Our lives sometimes have problems
And we know not always why,
Lord Jesus there to lead us
Through His Power there on High.

Thank Jesus for your problems
For in your weakness they feel wrong,
It is then through your weakness
Jesus' strength will make you strong.

How Heavenly

How Heavenly He calls to me,
Lord Jesus Christ, God's Gift for me
How Heavenly He softly calls my name.

He fills my life with love and grace,
He of no sin who took my place
Glory to the Father who sent His Son for me.

Oh Heavenly how great the cost,
That we of sin would not be lost
How Heavenly, My Savior's love for me.

With all my love I praise His name,
Within His love I'm not the same
His Word the daily guide for me.

Upon His cross I died to sin,
But yet through Christ I'm born again
Hallelujah to Lord Jesus Christ the King.

Oh Heavenly His Kingdom come,
And with my life His Will be done
The Holy One, Lord Jesus Christ in me.

Eternally I pray to be,
With Jesus Christ who rescued me
And evermore there with God's Trinity.

Guide My Words

Forgive me dear Lord Jesus
The sinner that I am,
Let my sins be all forgiven
And be no more a sinful man.

Forgive me for the times
I try to go my way,
Take my hand lead me back
Where on your path I kneel to pray.

Forgive me Lord for any day
I forget to praise your Name,
I love you my Lord Jesus
You have released my soul of shame.

Jesus all the words in me
To many sometimes I use,
Please Spirit guide my mouth
That worthless words I use be few.

Let all my words within
Be used to praise God's Holy Name,
Through Jesus Christ my Savior
With Newborn Life I Live again.

With this Newborn Life
And the Grace the Father gives,
The words I have are not enough
To Glorify my God who Lives.

Sing Praise

Oh hear my song Lord Jesus
Of your love and how it's felt,
I set here with no music
So I will sing the words myself.

I love you so Lord Jesus
You gave your Life that I may live,
Resurrected by the Father
Eternal Life to you He give.

Every day with you Lord Jesus
I pray my day with you not end,
And as I feel Your presence
My love for You I send.

You're the reason of God's Glory
You're the Prince our Lord the King,
With the thought of You Lord Jesus
To praise Your Name my heart must sing.

Please hear my song Lord Jesus
Hear the words I sing to You,
You are the one God's Holy Son
In You I live brand-new.

You fill my day with wonder
With joy You fill my heart,
Thank you dear Lord Jesus
I pray from You I never part.

Thank You

I am blessed again this morning
As Father opened up my eyes,
He gently wakes me from my sleep
In the bed in which I lie.

I thank him for the peaceful sleep
As He held me through the night,
He watched me and sustained me
Through the night unto the light.

I thank him for the breath that's there
For the beating of my heart,
Upon my knees beside my bed
I pray from him I never part.

I thank Him for the day ahead
And all the things He leads me to,
I thank Him for within my mind
I hear, I give my love to you.

His hand so gently leads me
To where He only knows,
And through the day I move along
As He shows me where to go.

My God I am so blessed by Thee
You are always by my side,
When sin and danger do come near
I run to You and in Your arms I hide.

Closing Thought

May the Blessings from Lord Jesus
Be Given You Each Day
May His Loving arms surround you
As you kneel to Him to pray.

Across the Jordan to Many Treasures

He is risen, He is risen,
Our Lord Jesus Christ the King,
His endless love and great mercy,
Forgives our sins then peace to us He brings.

Though the sins we have are many,
Give those sins to Jesus everyone,
Ask all your sins be forgiven,
Through Jesus Christ the Father's will be done.

God's love is wider than this universe,
God has forgiveness for all our sins,
Believe and ask Jesus to forgive,
God's open arms will surely draw you in.

There in the body, Jesus Christ
God's Holy Spirit to lead us every day,
Let your soul be raised to Almighty God,
Through Jesus Christ, God's Son, our only way.

What glory will be on that day,
Eternity will be ours, a day will be no more,
We too shall cross the Jordan, to God's Promised Land
To see the many treasures God has for us in store.

All Praise

All praise be to my God
All praise be unto Him,
All praise be to the living God
Who forgives me of my sins.

All praise be to God's goodness
All praise and fame be to His name,
All praise be to His faithfulness
Who each day stays just the same.

All praise be to my Father God
All praise to Him who watches over me,
All praise to Him who lights my way
That on His path I clearly see.

All praise be to my God
All praise be to His Son He sent for me,
All praise to Him upon that cross
There crucified to set me free.

All praise be to my Father
All praise to Jesus resurrection,
From the tomb to life then to ascension
Oh praise our Lord the King.

All praise to my Father God
Who gave His Son for me,
I give to You all praise and glory
Forevermore my God You'll be.

Almighty Power, All Caring Love

All power is my God
Almighty is His name,
From whence He came a mystery
Evermore eternally the Lord my God will reign.

Go out tonight raise your eyes above
Look up at all you see,
What you see is infinitesimal
Of the Glory of God there be.

Uncountable as the stars above
Is the vastness of the Lord my God the King,
Countless worlds and galaxies
Made He my God all things.

God made a man of this earth
In God's image was He to be,
God then breathed life into His lungs
God's friend this man was made sin free.

So man would not be alone
God with man's rib made for man a wife,
God made their bodies not the same
So their bodies could unite for creation of new life.

We all know the story
How Adam and Eve ate from the forbidden tree,
God said through their act of disobedience
Man would no longer be sin free.

Thousands of years later
God through Mary sent Lord Jesus Christ His Son,
To live upon this earth as man
The teaching life of Christ had now begun.

His words were from the Father
A guide to life that we should live,
Through His love and countless miracles
It was from the Father for Him to freely give.

Tortured whipped and beaten
Man then nailed Him to a cross,
Christ asked Father please forgive them
So their souls might not be lost.

At the foot of my Lord Jesus' cross
I look up and my heart does cry,
To know that because of me my sin
God's Son Lord Jesus had to die.

Almighty God so powerful
What great love God gave to us that day,
God's one begotten Son His blood for our salvation
Now through Christ must be our way.

God raised His Son from His tomb of death
My Lord is alive forevermore,
Now lives Christ with God the Father
Life with the Father is Jesus Christ salvations only door.

Glory hallelujah for the resurrection of the king
Through Jesus Christ God's will be done,
My heart that cried does now rejoice
Salvation through Jesus Christ has just begun.

Are You Ready?

Are you ready for Lord Jesus
If He returns to earth today,
Lord Jesus is coming back
And He is not that far away.

If this be the day God has chosen
For our Savior Christ's return,
Will you be with Him in Heaven
Or the lake of fire to ever burn.

The Father God so loves you
He leaves the choice there in your hands,
Confess all your sins to Jesus
And obey our God's commands.

Let Jesus come and touch your heart
His blood will wash away your sins,
You'll be then with God through Jesus
Resurrection God's gift to you through Him.

I pray through my Lord Jesus Christ
You not take the chance these words be wrong,
Make the choice be our Lord Jesus
Or burn throughout eternity, eternity be very long.

A Matter of Life

Father, God in Heaven
Has our life come down to this,
That the color of a man
Should be the reason he exists.

I know that You, my Father
Make your children many ways,
With many different colors
And different shapes and things to say.

God, I'll make this simple
The thing I have to say,
It's not the color of the skin that matters
That makes all life precious every day.

No matter the color of the skin
It's the person there inside,
The love and life placed in him
The skin's color cannot hide.

Attentive

Why does not my God talk to me
How many times I've said these words,
I pray to Him and call His name
But yet His voice I have not heard.

I read His Word on every day
On my knees to Him I pray,
I seek to see His face
And His voice my name to say.

How wonderful and good is my God
Who watches over me and guides my way,
My God is always with me
Someday in His voice my name He'll say.

But wait I may be reasoning
In a way that I should not,
Does not His word speak clear to me
My trust in Him there be my lot.

Every step that I do take
Jesus Christ walks there with me,
When my steps may lead to danger
Does not God's voice then caution me.

When I see someone in need
Does not God speak to me and say,
Be helpful to those in need
Do not turn and walk away.

Forgive me, God, my Father
For the error of my way,
I should be more attentive
As you talk to me each day.

That little voice within me
God I know that voice is You,
The tender voice that lights my way
To keep Your path for me in view.

If you think God does not talk to you
You are in error to think that way,
Watch close and be attentive
You'll see He talks to you each day.

A Special Day

God made my birthday special
It is the date and not the year,
The birthdate of my love, my Ronnie
Her date was yet away two years.

We're both born on the same day
Though we were born two years apart,
As a teen first I met her
And on that day she stole my heart.

She filled my heart with love for her
Her tender heart to be so clear,
Great joy she had within her
Great to me to have someone so dear.

All our years together
We shared our birthday everyone,
A special day God made for us
To celebrate and have some fun.

Another birthday comes upon me
The birthdate is still hers and mine,
But Father God has called her home
A way to celebrate sometimes is hard to find.

She has gone ahead of me to heaven
To be with our Father God,
I'm left here with great memories
I thank her and thank my God.

I pray someday we'll be together
But that day I know not when,
A special day God will give us
That special day that has no end.

Beauty

How many things of beauty
Has God made for us to see,
From amazing fields of grass
To the Glory of His trees.

A sky that's filled with puffy clouds
To seas of water oh so blue,
With animals of every sort
To show His wondrous love for you.

With all these things of beauty
And how beautiful all they are,
I submit to you another
More beautiful than a painting by Renoir.

When I look upon this beauty
It is absolutely clear to me,
That a woman bearing child
Is a most lovely site to see.

With such beauty in her eyes
Filled with joy and oh so clear,
In her eyes you see the love
For the child she holds so dear.

The beauty of her face
As she moves forward to the day,
Every day that beauty grows
God's love to show her way.

Through God you see the beauty
In her new life has come to be,
God's Holy hand of beauty
Rests on her for all to see.

Thank you God we see her beauty
Your loving hand does hold her near,
To me she is so lovely
That in my eye she brings a tear.

Christ Our Gift

How loving is the Father God
That gives His Grace to us each day,
Who sent His one begotten Son
To save us all from sinful ways.

He sent His Son Lord Jesus
To be a savior for us all,
To teach us more of Father God
And harken to His call.

His Son our Lord Jesus Christ
Gave us guidance how to pray,
Now His Spirit in us
That Spirit guides us what to say.

Is there any way for us to know
His forgiving awesome love,
For his creation he calls man
Than through Lord Jesus sent from God above.

A great and loving sacrifice
Father gave there for all man,
To see His Son upon a cross
With nails pierced through His feet and hands.

Crucified upon a wooden cross
His blood spilled there for all mankind,
He wore a crown of bloodstained thorns
Jesus Christ God's sacrificial Lamb.

He bore our sins upon that cross
His blood washed our sins away,
The glory of His resurrection
Those who call have newborn life
And live eternal life through Jesus every day.

Crucified

They knew not our Lord and Savior
Jesus Christ the Father's Son,
He who came to save this world
His Word the Father's Chosen One.

Unseeing eyes looked on Him
Covered ears heard not His word,
With hearts of stone they knew no love
His words of love they never heard.

In the garden called Gethsemane
His persecution there began,
Asked by the priest are you the Son of God
Lord Jesus answered, "That I am."

Accused and tried of blasphemy
His sentence was that He should die,
They spit on Him and mocked Him
A crown of thorns to support their lie.

Unmercifully they scourged Him
Whips that cut deep into His skin,
His body bruised and bloody
His trip to Calvary now begins.

His cross He bore upon His back
As they led Him up that hill,
They spit and kicked and beat Him
He went forth to do the Father's will.

High upon a hill called Calvary
On His cross they laid Him down,
They nailed His hands and feet to His cross
And then raised Him from the ground.

As He hung there on that cross
And asked Father, "Why have you forsaken me?"
We should try to understand
The reason sometimes we do not see.

As God turned His face from His Son
His face was turned to His creation man,
He sacrificed His one begotten Son
To show His love for man, our God, The Great I Am.

All our sins God placed on Him
The ones before and those to come,
When Jesus cried it is finished
His work upon the cross was done.

They laid Him in His tomb
He laid as sin God made of Him,
To pay our cost in the depth of hell
And there in hell He left our sins.

On the third day God raised Him up from His tomb
To be evermore at His right hand,
With Jesus' blood and belief in Him
The sins of ours no longer stand.

Our Lord and savior Jesus Christ
Our Father's Son He lives again,
Please my Father God
Make me pure as pure as Him.

Do Good

Do good, a very simple statement
Do good, as you live your life today,
Do good, hold the hand of Jesus
Do good, as He leads you on your way.

Do good, to those that are in need
Do good, help them as you may,
Do good, from the time the sun comes up
Do good, to all throughout the day.

Do good, to your sister and to your brother
Do good, show them that you care,
Do good, give to them your hand in friendship
Do good, your loved filled heart with them do share.

Do good, to all God's little children
Do good, of our Lord Christ Jesus teach them every day,
Do good, that they will know the man called Jesus
Do good, show them to our God, Lord Jesus is our way.

Do good, to everyone you meet
Do good, show to them your twinkling smile,
Do good, compliment them the best you can
Do good, see as they return your smile.

Do good, it is the way of Jesus
Do good, help your fellow man,
Do good, show that you love Jesus
Do good, through Jesus Christ I know you can.

A Time of Giving

The month that is December
A very special time it be,
An awesome day December twenty-five
The birth of our Savior sent for you and me.

A special time of giving love
On the birthday of our King,
To show our love for our God
And praise His name through songs in which we sing.

How great the love God gives to all
As He walks and talks with us each day,
His gift of love He works through us
In things we do and what we say.

Be cheerful in your giving
Through the Spirit's warmth that is within,
The Birthday of Lord Jesus Christ
Sent to free us of our sins.

How great the joy of giving
Great tears of joy become a part,
Of the knowledge it is God's love
That fills and overflows your heart.

May the feeling of free giving
Fill your heart on every day,
With love the Holy Spirit
Will then lead you on your way.

Forever the Word

As it was in the beginning
It is today and evermore shall be,
The Word of God my Father
Is His loving guide to me.

With His Word He made all that is
The greatness of the shining stars above,
With His Word then made this earth
Our home He made for us with love.

It was His Word He sent to earth
To be born here as a man,
To save the world and know of God
To love the One The Great I Am.

But evil men with sinful hearts
With darkened eyes that would not see,
They would not hear with covered ears
The Word of truth to set us free.

They scourged Him with their cruel whips
Placed a crown of thorns upon His head,
They spit on Him and mocked Him
As He bore His cross to where they led.

The Word called our Lord Jesus
Evil men hung there on a tree,
On Jesus' cross God's Will fulfilled
Jesus died as sin to set us free.

As it was in the beginning
It is today and evermore shall be,
Though they killed the man, Lord Jesus
They could not kill God's Word upon that tree.

Forever with Jesus

My life began forever
High upon that hill,
Where Jesus Christ my Savior
Died to fulfill the Father's will.

I kneel to Him upon His cross
There to thank Him as I pray,
For His sacrifice He gave for me
And gave His life to pay my way.

Never am I worthy
For the grace He gives each day,
But divinely through His blood
He has washed my sins away.

He guides my feet along His path
And lights the path that I may see,
It is His tender forgiving love
And His truth that sets me free.

All Glory to my Father God
Who sent His Son for me,
And bled and died on that cross
On that hill called Calvary.

Now through His resurrection
Belief in Him I'm born again,
To live with Him in heaven
When my life on earth does end.

God's Physician

I sit here this morning
The thoughts of Jesus fill my mind,
From his miracle conception
To the grown man that is so kind.

From His Sermon on the Mount
To the thousands upon the hill he fed,
His miracle with two fishes
And with only five loaves of bread.

His miracles of great healing
Of the lepers, the deaf, the blind,
All ills that came before Him
He left them not behind.

He taught throughout the Holy Land
To live through Him in faith and not the law,
In the law we could not move from sin
But faith in Christ removes it all.

He is the Father's great physician
The first heart transplant performed by Him,
He took away our cold, cold heart
To give us one tender and free from sin.

God's Word! New Day! Same Way!

Open up God's Holy Book
Read and hear what He has to say,
God's Word spoke from the start
Still applies to us today.

In the beginning God created man and woman
To be bound together as just one,
To be a friend of God's and bring forth new life
And to obey our God the Holy One.

The evil one brought forth temptation
On that day the sin of man began,
Their sin God's Word they did not obey
Now sin be born in every man.

God sent for us a Savior
His Son pure and without sin,
Sacrificed for our sin upon a cross
Washed in His blood we are only saved by Him.

Jesus Christ gave to us His warning
Of the evil ones that lay ahead,
Do not be lead into the darkness
Believe God's Word and hear what He has said.

The Word of God is written
In his Word the die is cast,
Truth be in his Word
From the beginning to the last.

Today there are those among us
Who would subvert God's Holy Word,
Heed not the words of those that say
Believe not what you have heard.

Follow not the Prince of Darkness
That man be with man as wife,
Or a woman have woman for a husband
Obey God live not that sinful life.

Heed not the words of those who say
The meaning of God's Word has changed,
Now their interpretation good is bad, and bad is good
The meaning of God's Word they try to rearrange.

This really tells the story how man does go astray
How the evil in this world will tempt us,
To live in sin and not obey
If God's Word you not obey, God's judgement will be just.

Through His Word as it is written
Live your life that Him you will obey,
Jesus Christ the Son of God shall return
I pray to be with Jesus on that day.

Guidance

Inside me speaks a little voice
That speaks in a powerful way,
It's the Spirit of my Lord Jesus
And He speaks to me each day.

As I lay in bed there still asleep
That gentle voice says open up your eyes,
A brand-new day I've made for you
Rejoice don't let it pass you by.

As I stir and then do arise
I hear the voice so softly say,
Be humble to the Father
Upon your knees now to Him pray.

The voice speaks very clearly
In Father's book go hear His Word,
The voice so present in my mind
As I read in His voice the word is heard.

And as my day does move along
And there is evil I cannot see,
The voice says, "No, no don't go that way
Hold My hand and follow Me."

Now I know if I heed that voice
To great things He'll show my way,
His voice most surely tells me
I'll be with Father God someday.

Healing Well

Lord my God my Father Creator of us all
All Mighty strength and power be in Your name.
Your gentle loving tenderness
Our very life each day in You sustained.

Through Your Son our Lord and Savior Jesus Christ
Your gift a sacrifice to save our souls from sin.
His loving work upon His cross
His life His blood He gave so we might win.

All those in need of healing
Drink from this well Jesus Christ be His name.
All waters from this blessed well
Heals the sick, the blind, the lame.

Even though we be not worthy of His Grace
In any works that we can do,
It is through Him alone Lord Jesus Christ
Belief in Him that brings new born life in you

How a Poem!

As I sit down with a pad and pen
I write out words that fill my mind,
The words start freely flowing
The words I write begin to rhyme.

The words be of the Spirit
Oh my God that lives in me,
I read the Father's Words
But there are times I do not see.

Times in early morning
The Spirit awakens me,
Get your pen and your paper
Write these words you did not see.

In my mind His words become a poem
In the poem a message there for me,
The message in the poem
Shows the words I did not see.

Now when the words I read
Be not completely clear I see,
The Spirit comes and wakens me
To give His Word and love to me.

I Walk on His Path

Let me walk down Your path
Jesus walk it with me,
Let me hold Your sweet hand
In Your truth keep me free.

As we walk down Your path
You're the Word to show me Your way,
I know You're with me
In my heart as I pray.

You're the one from the Father
Lord save me from sin,
You bled and died on that cross
In new life Father raised You again.

You're my light that is life
In my heart You're pure love,
In my mind You give peace
You're my God from above.

I love You sweet Jesus
You're the living Spirit in me,
I thank You Lord Jesus
That saved a sinner like me.

Intercede

Please my Lord and Savior Jesus Christ
Hear my words as I kneel to You to pray,
Please take my prayer to Father God
That He may hear me as I pray.

Please Lord Jesus intercede for me
For Lord it is only You that can,
Please make clear to God the words I say
Humbled I pray to my God the sinner that I am.

Please Jesus my prayer to Father God
Sweet blessings for my family one and all,
I pray that God will touch their hearts
And touch their ears to hear His call.

Please Jesus You know all my friends
I pray God's blessings for them all,
Those of them who are weak and ill
Please Jesus hold their hand so they not fall.

Please Jesus I pray to God for those in need
Their numbers seem to grow on every day,
Father God I know You see their needs
Guide me God so I may help them in some way.

Please Jesus I pray to God for this land
I pray this country will not fall,
I pray You give a warning of our great sin
That we may see and heed Your call.

Please Jesus I pray for the unborn child
God change the minds of those who take their lives,
God I pray all abortions be aborted
And all Your children have a chance to live their lives.

A prayer for me Lord Jesus is kind of hard to say
Father God is so good to me on every day,
My prayer to God is give me strength
Please God do Your work through me every day in any way.

Through You my Lord Jesus Christ I pray
Intercede to God for me, my prayers to Him I say.

Jesus Love Prayer

Jesus You are the goodness
I seek out every day,
What compassion fills Your eyes
As I kneel to You to pray.

I know that I am loved by You
As I know You are loved by me,
I read Your Words on every day
Your Words to guide that I may see.

Your Love for me consumes my soul
You give my heart the will to love,
My heart and soul I give to You
You are my only Lord, my peaceful snow-white dove.

Your shining light oh Jesus
I pray that shining light's in me,
I pray someday to be like You
And all will see that part of You in me.

Please Jesus may it be Your Will
The love You give will pass through me,
Within Your love You give me strength
So help me Lord to be the best that I can be.

What love the Father shows to me
That I may share His only Son,
Who gave His Blood and Life for me
And eternal life for me He won.

Lead Me

Please God, my Father in Heaven
Hear my voice I raise to You, Lord, in prayer,
Please accept my words, I lay here before You
I know my God is always there.

I pray for Your guidance, down the path that You lead me
I pray from that path, I go not astray,
On Your path, let my feet never stumble
Let my vision, be only of You every day.

Please, my Lord, my God in Heaven
With Your love fill my heart, so there is no despair,
Fill my mind, with Your loving forgiveness
All that You give, let me with others then share.

Let the sins of my past, be no more remembered
What lay ahead, be it all praise to Your Name,
Through Your Son, my Savior Lord Jesus
I am born once again, thank You, God, that He came.

Love, Attention, and Praise

Lord my God in Heaven hear me as I pray
Is there a way I may say thank You,
That I have not said before this day
I seek words to say I love You, and thank You as I pray.

At the time of my conception
Your gentle hands were there with me,
Within my mother's womb You formed me
With a loving plan for me to be.

Thank You God for loving me
Even when I sinned and went astray,
Thank You for the newness in my life
That You give to me each day.

Thank You for the sun above
That is our light throughout the day,
Thank You for the air we breathe
Thank You for Your Spirit to guide our way.

Thank You for the moon above
In the night that gives us light,
Thank You for the shining stars in heaven
That sparkle like diamonds in the night.

Thank You for all the life You give
With such abundance in the air, land, and sea,
Thank You for Your works of beauty
Made with loving hands for all to see.

Thank You for the one You sent to save this world
Your Son Lord Jesus Christ to show Your way,
Crucified upon the cross, Lord Jesus,
His blood spilled on us to wash our sins away.

I thank You God my Father
Till my life on earth is through,
Then evermore in heaven
I'll give thanks to be forever there with You.

Mirror, Mirror

When you look into a mirror
What is it there you see,
Of course you say it is myself
The person in that mirror is me.

Now what if you looked into my mirror
Instead of you, you there saw me,
How would we tell the difference,
That makes you you and makes me me?

What if that in this world
We all looked just the same,
If we could not tell anyone apart
Then what good would be a name?

You were not born from a mold
But you were formed with loving care,
With loving hands God formed you
He made you one and not a pair.

Though sometimes two may look alike
There within they're not the same,
One may be very humble
And the other reach out for fame.

So when you look into your mirror
You are but one and never two,
God made that special thing in that mirror
And that special thing is you.

Now the appearance of the outer shell
Is not important no not at all,
It's the specialness of difference
That makes one short the other tall.

God put within the outer shell
A person with a loving heart,
He knows the person in that shell
He knew all about them from the start.

Remember now that God made you
He made you one that is all new,
God's hands makes only special things
And that special thing He made is you.

My Bride

Another year has come and gone
That my bride is no longer at my side,
I held her hand in mine till her last breath
Then in sorrow I hung my head and cried.

Yet memories are always with me
I see her face and feel her love,
Though she be not here at my side
She is with my Father God above.

All memories and they be many
Gentle and so kind she my loving wife,
Her cheerful laugh a smile comes to my face
She always is my love, my bride, my life.

As I held her hand and she slipped away
I felt a special part of me was gone,
How joyful would it be,
If we could dance again one song?

She is at home with Father God
Now she has been there for six years,
Each and every memory
Brings sometimes a smile, sometimes a tear.

My God

In the presence of the Lord
I fall humbly to my knees,
To Him I am so thankful
He who saved a wretch as me.

The Lord my God my Father
Filled with love and Grace He gives,
Through His Son my Lord and Savior
Upon His cross died that I might live.

He is my God that is filled with goodness
He is my God filled with love for me,
He is my God who gives His Word of truth
He is my God who gave His Word for me.

Each and every day He leads me to
Of worldly things I see them change,
But every day within my heart
My God of love remains the same.

Never leaves He me alone
In my heart and soul He is always there,
He teaches me to love and forgive
And what I have that I should share.

Lord God You are so beautiful
As I kneel before You in prayer,
Help me God that I tell others
Of Your love and how much You care.

My God, My Jesus, My Spirit

I thank my God the Father
Who sustains me through the night,
Who loves and watches over me
All through the night unto the light.

As I lay me down and close my eyes
And blissful sleep comes over me,
The Spirit of my Father's Son
Gently rocks the cradle He made for me.

All my dreams He sees them
He sees the bad and alters them to good,
While I sleep He works His wonders
That I will follow Him the way I should.

As the new day comes
He gently calls me to awake,
Come see the day I've made for you
First say your prayers and this day will be just great.

I thank my God upon my knees
He who is loving and so kind,
While I was yet deep in sin
Jesus held out His hand for me to find.

Christ bled and died on His cross for me
In Jesus' blood my sins washed clean,
Every sin nailed to His cross
Now all dead and can't be seen.

They laid Him in a tomb
Three days He paid my cost,
Through His resurrection I be born again
Thank God I am not lost.

As this day comes to an end
I pray to my God again,
He who gives me peaceful restful sleep
With His love and with sweet dreams.

My Prayer

Lord, I give You all praise now and forever
God, only in You is thy Holy name,
Your Name Lord to me the Highest of Highest
The breadth of Your love and the length of Your fame.

God, You have made all we see here before us
From the depth of Your sea,
To the heights of Your heavens above
Someday I pray Your face I shall see.

You sent us Your Son Lord Jesus our Savior
Who went to His cross to save us from sin,
You took all our sins and placed them upon Him
He bled and died on His cross to forgive all our sins.

When I have sinned and fallen short of Your glory
When I am down and fear all is lost,
Lord, lift me up as if on wings of an eagle
Raise me up to the Foot of His cross.

At the Foot of His cross I ask for forgiveness
I pray through His blood He will wash all my sins,
Jesus, only in You has all power been given
To clean all my sins and take me safely to Him.

Look to the Scriptures

I can listen to your problems
I can have compassion for what they be,
I can pray that Jesus helps you
But your answer is not in me.

Consider what is your problem
Seek ye help in a faithful hand,
Turn ye to the scriptures
Your answer be in Him the Great I AM.

So many places in His Book
His love to lead your way,
Isaiah 41:10 for you a passage
To help you with your problem on this day.

Fear not is God's instructions
That you may put all trust in Him,
In the book of Psalms 139:9–10 and 11
His Words there as a beautiful lovely hymn.

The book of John chapter 14 to you the verse 18
As you read these words you will know,
The love of Christ is with you
No matter when or where you go.

My Talk with Jesus

As I wake up every morning
To the day that lay ahead,
I think of my Lord Jesus
Who my God raised from the dead.

I say my prayers to Jesus
On my knees beside my bed,
I pray to my Lord Jesus
Guide my day to where I'm led.

I look for Him He's here with me
My life is in His hands,
I found my way to talk with Him
It's through the Bible that I can.

I read the Words He wrote to me
And when sometimes the Words not clear,
He'll come to me and touch my ears
That what I see, I also hear.

To read His Word I talk with Him
I want His way to be my way,
And when I have a question
I wait to hear what He will say.

And when Lord Jesus answers me
The answer is his Word,
With my eyes I see His answer
And with my ears His answers heard.

I thank You Lord Jesus
For my time with You each day,
Thank You for forgiveness
And a bright new special day.

I thank You my Lord Jesus
For all the goodness that is You,
Thank You for the Blood You shed
Through Your Blood I'm born brand-new.

Never-Ending Thank You

As you wake up every morning
To the new day that Jesus made,
Thank Him for His life He give
Our debt for sin upon the cross He paid.

There should be a thank you in the morning
There should be thank you through the day,
Every time you think of Him
Just kneel and thank Him as you pray.

Thank Him for His forgiveness
Thank Him for the love He gives to you,
Thank Him for so many things
Thank Him for the old and for the new.

Thank Him for the old
The man that once was you,
Thank Him for the new
The newborn man He made of you.

And when sometimes
There be a problem in your day,
Know that Jesus sees it
So thank Him anyway.

We could not list all blessings
From Jesus Christ that all have came,
The list would be ten thousand miles long
And then ten thousand miles again.

Every breath it be a blessing
And every beat with in your heart,
A thank you always on our lips
To pray from Christ we never part.

On Calvary

On Calvary,
On Calvary,
Upon that cross
Christ died for me.
Stands a cross on Calvary
Where Jesus died for me.
His blood stains the cross
Where He paid my cost
On that hill called Calvary.
On Calvary,
On Calvary,
Jesus Christ
There died for me.
He took my place
On that cross,
To rescue me
On that hill called Calvary.
Oh Lord my God
What has man done,
They crucified
Thy Holy Son.
The Prince of Peace
The Father's Son,
The Lamb of God
Thy will be done.
He died for me
Upon that tree,
Now through His Blood
I am set free

On that hill called Calvary.
On Jesus Christ
My Lord and King
It is through You
My life begins.
The sacrifice
You paid for me
That Bloodstained cross
On Calvary.
The Symbol of Redeeming Grace
A crown of thorns
Amazing Grace.
You took my sins
Upon Your cross,
You left them there
You paid my cost.
On Calvary,
On Calvary,
Upon Your cross
You rescued me
On that hill called Calvary.

Only This Day

Our life upon this earth
A tick upon the clock of time,
How fleeting and how short it is
For I be a sinner as is all mankind.

A thought came to waken me
As I lay asleep in bed,
Of all my sins of yesterdays
And fear of what may lay ahead.

The Spirit came to tell me
Yesterday's sins you have already spent,
And if there be tomorrow
Upon your knees repent.

The things that are of yesterdays
I cannot change at all,
But live to God all this day
And if tomorrow it is the Father's call.

In heaven is no yesterdays
Tomorrow there is no need you see,
For through our Lord Jesus Christ
This day with God is all we need.

When we pass from this life
And to God's kingdom we come,
Of time there will be no more need
Yesterday, tomorrow, and today are all one.

Perfect Love

In awe I set and wonder
Who am I that God should even care,
Then I feel His Words upon my heart
You are my child for you always I'll be there.

How perfect is the love of our God
In Awesome Glory displayed each day,
From the air I breathe to my heart that beats
Countless blessings God gives to me in many ways.

In pureness His Son Lord Jesus Christ
God's Word to teach man that live in sin they must repent,
He died upon a cross to save our souls
To do the Father's Will the reason He was sent.

Now every day as I go on my way
My guide, the Light I have inside,
God's Holy Spirit now lives in me
In the Holy Trinity I now am Sanctified.

On Calvary

On Calvary,
On Calvary,
Upon that cross
Christ died for me.
Stands a cross on Calvary
Where Jesus died for me.
His blood stains the cross
Where He paid my cost
On that hill called Calvary.
On Calvary,
On Calvary,
Jesus Christ
There died for me.
He took my place
On that cross,
To rescue me
On that hill called Calvary.
Oh Lord my God
What has man done,
They crucified
Thy Holy Son.
The Prince of Peace
The Father's Son,
The Lamb of God
Thy will be done.
He died for me
Upon that tree,
Now through His Blood
I am set free

On that hill called Calvary.
On Jesus Christ
My Lord and King
It is through You
My life begins.
The sacrifice
You paid for me
That Bloodstained cross
On Calvary.
The Symbol of Redeeming Grace
A crown of thorns
Amazing Grace.
You took my sins
Upon Your cross,
You left them there
You paid my cost.
On Calvary,
On Calvary,
Upon Your cross
You rescued me
On that hill called Calvary.

Promised Land

Thank You Lord my God
That through Your Son You hear my plea,
Thank You for Your Guiding Light
Thank You for Your Son who rescued me.

I read how when in Egypt Your chosen people
Were held in bondage four hundred fifty years,
In a burning bush You called Your servant Moses
To rid them of their burden and relieve them of their fears.

You used Your servant Moses
To free them from the bondage of Pharaoh's hand,
Your mighty arm stretched out through Moses
You brought them out of Egypt to journey to Your Promised Land.

I see that in this world
An evil Prince of Darkness has his way,
When You gave Your Son Lord Jesus Christ
Through Him the evil prince was defeated on that day.

Your Son our Lord and Savior Jesus Christ
Upon His cross died so we might live forever more,
Within His tomb God gave Him eternal life
Lives the King of Kings now and evermore.

Our Lord Jesus Christ will return again
To free believers from Satan's sinful hand,
And as God's mighty arm stretched out through Moses
In Jesus Christ we will journey to Your Promised Land.

Pure Love

O Lord my God
This special poem I write to You,
Thank You for Your Son Lord Jesus
So I could be born again all new.

All in all my God is pure love
Who sustains and watches over me,
As on the wings of His snow-white dove
It is God's pure love that raises me.

Tender yet almighty the everlasting God
Your Son Lord Jesus Christ King of all the Kings,
Gives witness God to Your majesty
Humble and obedient to the Father in all things.

His Blood, His life, He gave it all
To do Lord God the Father's will,
Made sin to die upon a cross on Calvary
To forgive our sins there high upon that hill.

Goodness love and majestic is our God
Gave new life to His Son within His tomb,
Through Christ Jesus I too can have new life
Our savior Jesus Christ is coming back quite soon.

Received

Jesus Christ my Lord Jesus Christ
From Father God to earth You came,
You God's Word divinely sent
To Glorify the Father's Holy Name.

You the One begotten Son of Father God
Sent here to save a world of sin,
Our Savior Christ of Almighty God
That belief in You we may live again.

Your Word, Your Touch, Your Loving Care,
To teach us all in You should be our way,
You reach down in and touch the hearts
Of God's children who have gone astray.

Almighty is the Son of God
And loving kindness is His way,
Through Your Spirit here inside
I feel these words that I should say.

At the feet of You upon Your cross
Where Your Blood and life did pay my cost,
Let my life now live through You
In You I'm found, in You I'm never lost.

Return

Jesus Christ my Lord and King
On God's chosen day shall return for me,
There in the clouds Christ will to all appear
An angel's shout, a trumpet sound, for all to hear.
There will be Lord Jesus Christ for all of man to see.

In the darkness of this world
Are we preparing for that day,
Do we search for shining things of this world
Worldly things that shine then fade away.
Seek first the face of Jesus Christ our Lord the king.

There on a hill so long ago
Upon a cross God sacrificed His Son,
His Life the price that I be forgiven of my sins
My Savior died God raised Him then to life again.
We know where He will come but only God knows when.

Keep yourself from darkness in this world
Let love fill your heart allow no evil to come in,
Let your life emit the light of Christ
That all will know that you belong to Him.
Then in the clouds be with Him when He comes back again.

Sacrifice

Once a tomb held Jesus Christ
The Prince of Peace the Father's Son,
Our Savior sent to save this world
God's Holy Word God's chosen One.

Upon His cross He bled and died
As He fulfilled the Father's will,
With nails of iron and a crown of thorns
His sacrifice upon that hill.

Our Father God gave to us His Son
To die on a cross on Calvary,
Now with His death and through His blood
Belief in Him we are set free.

Lowered to His Mother Mary, down from His cross
Within her arms she held near her precious Son,
Great tears of sorrow fell on His face
Her Son of God the Holy One.

They took Him then to Joseph's tomb
They laid Him there to lay in rest,
For our sins three days in hell
His sacrifice so our lives could be the best.

Our Father God then called Him back
From death to life within that tomb,
The sting of death has been defeated
Lord Jesus Christ has Risen from that tomb.

He's alive, He lives evermore without an end
Through Him is heaven's open door,
Put your belief and trust in Him
To live with God forever more.

His Spirit lives within us
To guide our soul from dark into His light,
He is always there to guide our way
Never left alone were always in His sight.

Sister Mary Rose McGeady

Sister Mary Rose McGeady
God's vessel of love and unyielding faith,
Gives hope to homeless young children
Through their sorrow and sadness she saw God in their face.

Hurting, dirty, tired, and weary
Homeless young children with no place to go,
Sister Mary Rose McGeady
With loving arms brought them in from out of the cold.

A servant of God, a woman of love to behold
Gave of herself to homeless children unknown,
Sister Mary Rose McGeady
Her covenant house for homeless children a home.

Her great heart filled with love and compassion
With untiring arms to draw in her foal,
Sister Mary Rose McGeady
God's love through this woman, a great story told.

Speck of Life

Sometimes I ponder how great is my God
My God that has made all things that be,
All things that be a never-ending universe
Then in His love made a creature such as me.

Who am I but a speck of dust upon this earth
Given life by the Lord my God the King,
Life to be in His image
Body, soul, and Spirit gave God to me these three things.

A body that breathes life
A soul that sometimes goes astray,
A Spirit that lives within
To guide my soul on every day.

Lord Jesus Christ, God's lovely Son
My salvation only comes through Him,
Him, my God, sacrificed then in His tomb He rose again
To give to me eternal life and forgive me of my sins.

Thank you, God, I this tiny speck
For the life love and blessings that you give,
Your encouragement and Lord Jesus Christ
I stand tall through your love this life I live.

The Sabbath

Six days God performed His mighty works
Each day His works became complete,
Each day He looked and said it is good
Each day brought forth a new and awesome feat.

The seventh day God made is Holy
A day of rest to honor Him,
A day to lay aside our work
To worship Him and only Him.

I fear we have lost the meaning
Of this day of rest God gave to us,
This day the Holy Sabbath
To rest in God and therein our trust.

There be distractions all around us
Things that sometimes lead to sin,
Put our Father God before you
And give all honor unto Him.

All of those who are texting
Put away your phone give your thumbs a rest,
Set back and look around you
God made this all for you and made you His very best.

On God's Holy Day the Sabbath
Is it necessary to the mall you go,
Do you have to buy what is on sale
Or honor God and to that sale just say no.

On the Sabbath God's Holy Day
Is it must the TV's on?
Tune your mind to God and not that set
Till day is night and night is gone.

Within your six days before the Sabbath
Do your works that must be done,
Be observant of your commitments
And each day take time to have some fun.

God has given us so many things
To make our life more pleasant every day,
Now on this day the Sabbath
We honor Him and to Him we pray.

So keep the Sabbath Holy
Snuggle up there in God's hands,
Take a nap in restful sleep
To honor the one our only God the Great I AM.

The Seed

There is this little Seed
My Lord Jesus planted here in me,
His Word, His Seed, that I may hear
And when I hear His Seed then let's me see.

Lord Jesus with His Seed
Plants it deep within my soul,
There he gently nurtures it
So everyday His Seed can grow.

With tenderness and loving care
His Seed begins to grow,
Each day His Seed takes root
His Word, His Seed, to show me where to go.

As His Seed within me
Brings forth fruit which is His Light,
I pray His Light, His Seed, in me
Shines brightly day and night.

Let everyday His Seed please grow in me
I pray in me His Seed will shine so bright,
I pray His Word, His Seed, does fill my soul
That forevermore I shine brightly in His Light.

The Trumpets Call

The Prince of Peace, the King of Kings
The Lord and Master of us all,
How glorious that day shall be
To see our Lord, to hear the Trumpets Call.

He is Alive and well, He's coming back
So lend an ear and look above,
Pray to Him, the Word of God
God's Son who died for us to show His love.

The day Jesus Christ comes back again
That special day we know not when,
We will all stand before Lord Jesus Christ
And we shall bow and every knee will bend.

We worship God through Jesus Christ
God's Son resurrected in that tomb,
To a new and everlasting life
A new life born of God and not the womb.

How great will be the honor
To be in the presence of the King,
To kneel to Him upon His throne
To give all praise and to our Lord to sing.

Thank You Lord, God my Father
You are all that was, and is, and is to come,
You gave us life and a path to eternal life
Through Lord Jesus Christ, Your One Begotten Son.

The Water's Edge

As I walked along the path of life
A flood of waters blocked my way,
To the other side upon this path
I would not get there on this day.

I stood there with great yearning
That I might reach the other side,
In my mind I sought an answer
To reveal the way before my eyes.

I looked and saw another path
With a man there walking on,
He said come walk with me
For the path you' re on is wrong.

It was my Lord Jesus Christ
Across the waters led me that day,
He called me to walk upon His path
Now I'm on that path to stay.

He walks with me, He teaches me
He calls me back if I do wrong,
He's always right here with me
For His Love goes on and on.

Now as you walk your path of life
And great waters block your way,
Walk up to the water's edge
Don't turn and walk away.

Just look around you'll see a path
With a Man there walking on,
He will ask you then to follow Him
And leave that path that is all wrong.

Upon His path then walk with Him
Hold His hand to guide your way,
Now look ahead and don't look back
In Jesus Christ you're on His path to stay.

He will lead you across the waters
His Great Love for you so strong,
As you walk with Him upon His path
His Love will shield you from all wrong.

Those of Need

Blessed am I by the Lord my God
But let me not speak about things of me,
Let me speak of those afflicted
For it is God's child that He sees.

God knows of their affliction
And has His Godly plan for everyone,
We be included in that plan
Blessed by Jesus Christ the Father's Son.

With favor of the Father
Lord God chooses for us to be,
With compassion, aid, and comfort
For those afflicted wherever they may be.

Give of your hearts all filled with love
God gives love for one and all,
So when you see affliction
Then answer compassions call.

God knows of all afflictions
It's Father's plan we heed His call,
For we are all of God the Father
It is His will we love them all.

For all those that are afflicted
When Father God does call them home,
Father God will heal and make them whole
For God has left them not alone.

To Jesus

As I spend my time with Jesus
And we're alone just by ourselves,
He is a Special Warmth within me
He's the Love and Word that always helps.

He's the feeling deep within
That says I'm here right by your side,
I will be all day here with you
I will never leave your side.

He leads me in so many things
Sometimes there filled with fun,
I feel His joy within me
My Father's One Great Joyous Son.

As he leads me through the day
And something comes to cause a tear,
He wraps His arms around me
And then gently wipes away my tears.

As I seek a way to Praise Him
The Holy Spirit leads my way.
With His poems it's just like music
To Jesus Christ these words I say.

Trouble in Lust

Is there trouble in your life
Is that trouble caused from sin,
Do you celebrate some worldly lust
In that lust you think you win?

When lusting in sinful worldly things
With your life you'll lust for more,
The trouble caused from sinful lust
Cannot be hid behind a door.

So raise your hand to Jesus
His great peace He'll bring to you,
He'll reach down in your darkness
To become a shining light for you.

Be baptized with the water
Testify belief in Him,
Ask for His forgiveness
His blood washes away your sins.

Now the life you give to Jesus
He will not take away your lusts,
As you put all trust in. Him
He will take you away from them.

Up from the Valley

Lost in the valley, the valley of sin
I was there in great darkness,
Great sorrow within
A man of no peace and a man with no rest.

Then came forth Lord Jesus
The Shepard to find His lost sheep,
The Pure Light that is Life
Who raised me up from the deep.

His Blood on the cross
His Life He gave there for me,
To pay for my sins
Now raised from the dead with the Father is He.

Across the hills and the valleys
Walks this Shepard with me,
From the Lord God my Father
With great light that I see.

He is my Shepard of Goodness
And my Shepard of Love,
He guides and protects me
This Shepard my Lord from above.

Now I walk through the valleys
Over hills and through streams,
Within now great peace
And at rest with sweet dreams.

What a Day

Life is as a single day
As you waken to the morning light,
Your eyes open as when you were born
You remember not the dark of night.

There stands a bright new day before you
As a baby you have never seen before,
A day filled with many wonders
A new world to be explored.

A day that may bring a sorrow
To your eyes may cause a tear,
A day Christ gives His hand to you
Draws you close to relieve you of all fears.

A day our God has given to you
The only God who gave you life,
A fun-filled day you can enjoy
A day through Him that is so bright.

As the light of day begins to dim
When you feel it is time to rest
Your eyelids feel so heavy
You fall asleep there in your nest.

You sleep throughout the darkness
As in the tomb where Jesus lay,
He woke His Son from His sleep
He wakens us to His eternal day.

Why Man? Why Woman?

As God created man
From man's rib God created man a wife,
Therein He set in motion
A process for the conception of new life.

God's creations man and woman
He gave to man for new life His Seed,
And for new life made He the woman host
Different be their bodies but jointly be their needs.

Though God made their bodies not the same
Just stop and look it is plain to see,
That if it does not work God's way
Then today there would be no me.

God made not man to be man's spouse
Nor woman a spouse of a woman to be,
To God this is an abomination
Read in His Word in there you'll see.

Yet we love you as a brother
And sister we love you the same,
To our God we pray for you
That you not live that life of shame.

With God a New Day

How great will be this new day that is dawning
A new day that is made by my God the Father of all,
How clear in my eyes will I see His Love for me
As His Light fills my life and His Truth is my call.

How Glorious He fills each day with His Blessings
How tender His Hand as He leads me His way,
My needs through Him are most gladly given
Humbled on knees to my God do I pray.

With the Word of my Father
All things are created before me,
The air that I breathe to the blood in my veins
His Word that I hear, His great Beauty I see.

With my love for my Father, my God in Heaven
I place my life secure in Your Hands,
Please God use my life for Your Glory
Make changes in me as only You can.

With God in my life, no fear is before me
With God, my past I no longer see,
In the Blood of His Word my Savior Lord Jesus
Has washed all my sins and has set me free.

The Door

If you be in darkness
If your life be filled with sin,
Knock at the Door Lord Jesus Christ
He will wash away your sin then, He will call you in.

He is the faithful Door that is always there
For those in sin who've lost their way,
Call on Him, knock on that Door Lord Jesus Christ,
Opened then will be the Door to a bright new shining day.

A new day filled full with Jesus Christ
With new clothes as white as snow,
Filled with peace, love, and tranquility
In every direction you may go.

In Jesus Christ you will be in the Light of God
Our Father God His face you'll see O Holy be His Name,
A forever day called eternity a day that never ends
Eternal life with our God complete and without blame.

With God's Help!

If by the Will of God your days be many
And some parts not work so well,
Let's look upon what man has made
And what God has made the difference can you tell.

What of an auto made by man
Made on my day of birth,
With untold miles on every day
What would that car be worth?

With loving care and oil changed
When need new tires put on for feet,
At the most after fifteen years
That car would be cast upon a heap.

By the Grace of God my Father
Seventy-six years since my day of birth,
Yet still I have most of my hair
Extra pounds around my waist, whatever that is worth.

My arms and legs still function
Though not as smoothly as once they were,
With my eyes I still do see
If you speak up clearly my ears hear every word.

And with the nose upon my face
Sweet aromas still I smell,
As for my feet that once did run
Now runs my nose as well.

Now when nighttime comes
And bright stars come out for us to see,
So do the teeth within my mouth
For they don't belong to me.

In the morning as the new day comes
I pray to Jesus Christ the Father's Son,
When I rise and get to my feet
Jesus holds my hand and says let's go have some fun.

I Thank You, God, for all Your Blessings
And the great life You have given to me,
Oh and, God, just one more thing
I have a hip that bothers me.

Your Word

Father of Love as I read in Your Bible
All Your Words of wisdom You give,
I love You my God now and forever
Your Word and Your Love be my life that I live.

God how wonderful is Your Word and Your Glory
How mighty and kind is Your Love for us all,
Lord I pray as You look on us from Heaven
Your Spirit will lead us to You when You call.

How amazing is Your Word in Your Bible
How great the greatest of stories is told,
How wonderful it would be to be as a witness
To have lived back then to watch it unfold.

A body from dust Lord God You have given
This body of dust to dust it shall go,
Yet inside this body lives a soul and a spirit
Your Spirit that came to guide this poor soul.

A body unable to return and witness Your Story
But through Your Word in my mind it is told,
Thank You my God for Your changes within me
To live in Your story that never grows old.

Loving God

Another day has come from Lord God my Father
Granted to me, through his unending love,
All Glory and praise to my God, now and forever
Thankful am I, to my God up above.

A merciful God looks on me from Heaven
God's Eye, and His Hand, ever present with me,
Almighty God, has mercy forever and ever
I this sinner, humble myself unto Thee.

Your Spirit in me, o Lord God my Father
Let it grow in great strength, that I magnify Thee,
With your Spirit in me, o my Lord Jesus
Let the words from my mouth, speak only praise unto Thee.

Shout praise to my God, high in the mountains
The echo there of resound, in the land and the sea.
Speak oh my heart, of the love of the Father
Guide the life that I live, God only to Thee.

Give Me God's Word

Around me, there be so many earthly things
Some made of steel, some of wood, some of clay,
These things made to appear attractive
Things to be desired sometimes led my soul astray.

Earthly things, that are so tempting to my flesh
To my soul, they are an inanimate thing,
But the spirit, that is in me
Is that of Jesus Christ, my Lord, the King.

On my knees, praying to my God
I asked Lord, my God, what is it you want of me,
Then in my heart, I heard him say
You have my Word, read in there you'll see.

So give to me God's Holy Word
Let me read, and ponder it on every day,
Vast knowledge, and great wisdom
In God's Word, His love for all displayed.

The Evil Spirit Antichrist

There is an evil, building in this land
It is the spirit, of the Antichrist,
It is the evil plan, of Satan
To kill all belief, of our Savior Jesus Christ.

The pure evilness, of the Antichrist
Becomes more apparent, every day,
A government, the ruling class
Work to take the Word, our Lord Jesus Christ away.

They work hard to change the history, of our fathers
Who brought forth through God, this special land,
Endowed through God, with human rights
A Christian nation under God and protected by His hand.

The evil of the Antichrist is at work within our schools
Not only the Word, our Lord Jesus Christ they ban,
They forbid the Bible, to be read in school
And the pledge to our flag, they simply cannot stand.

As the daughter, of your mother
Who through God, did give your life to you,
When conception of creation, then occurs in you
Have you the right to kill, or be the mother, of the
Child that lives in you.

If you think it is your choice, for life or death
For the living being, there in your womb,
Abortion it be called, but murder is its, name
It is the spirit of the Antichrist, that is alive in you.

Those who swear an oath, to protect the human life
Some have forgotten their oath, and serve the evil Antichrist,
With evil hand's, they kill babies, that have for them no defense
Evil riches come to the hands, who serve the evil Antichrist.

The Antichrist is filled with darkness
That spirit gives no light for you to see,
His plan to keep you blind
To live in evil sin, not ever to be tree.

An abomination to God, that man have sex with man
Or woman, to do with woman, also the same,
The Antichrist puts forth a softer phrase, to be accepted
What they do is not sin, they are but simply gay.

We pray to fight the spirit, of the Antichrist
That God will show them, the sinfulness of their way,
Our Lord Jesus Christ will give them light
To be not blind but find our Savior's way.

For those unwed, that satisfy their lust in fornication
It is the spirit of the Antichrist, that tells your flesh to go ahead,
It is the spirit of the Antichrist who shows that lust to you
Reject the evil spirit Antichrist, seek our Savior Jesus Christ instead.

Fornication, just for fornication's sake, with anyone you choose
Only doom and death will be for you your reward,
Repent, confess your sins, to our Savior Jesus Christ
Be born again all new in Jesus Christ and live forever with the Lord.

Those who live together, as man and wife
But feel marriage, is not the life for you,
For man and woman, marriage is the Father's will
Do not allow the spirit of the Antichrist, to work in you.

If your love for one another does fill your heart
In marriage be bound together, and become as one,
With love commit your life to each other, until death does come
Your soul commit to God, through Jesus Christ, the Father's Son.

For all those who live in darkness
Reach out a hand to Jesus Christ, who is our light,
Let his spirit come live within you
So, we may put down, the evil Antichrist.

Light up your soul from darkness
Call to our Lord and Savior Jesus Christ,
Ask forgiveness, be granted you this day
The eternal door to Heaven is Jesus Christ our shining light.

Be tender, caring, loving, and forgiving
Try every day to help someone, reach out to take their hand,
The spirit of the Antichrist will try to block your way
But we all have power, and authority, in Jesus
Christ we all can stand.

If you be so foolish, to think this message does not apply to you
Look around, take assessment, of what you see, hear, say, and do,
If you read this message and see these things in your life
No longer be deceived, it is the spirit of the Antichrist in you.

For All to See

A rose of any color
What sweet aroma does fill the air,
Thorns upon its vine, to protect
The lovely flower, for all to share.

The awesome life, in God's creation
Molded, by the power of His Word,
From the roses, of many colors
To his bird, whose song is heard.

Great animals, that roam the plains
Fish and whales, that swim the sea,
Birds on wings that fly, and touch the sky
O what beauty, made for all to see.

His fields all lush, and o so green
His forest tall, with his majestic trees,
His fields filled, with lovely flowers
Upon those flowers, God's tiny bees.

A rose of any color
God made His children, also that way,
His loving hand does protect us
Lord God, we thank you, on our knees to you we pray.

Lord God, You are so wonderful
You are gentle and so kind,
Each day we see Your beauty
Each day, Your beauty fills our mind.

His Word

When I read His Word, in God's Holy Book
Each chapter and verse, as He speaks to me,
I pray for knowledge, and for great wisdom
What is His Word, my Father says unto me.

The treasured words, within God's Holy Book
Purposed to be read, and understand,
These words written by man, through the will of our Father
Words of wisdom, through God's mighty hand.

Our Almighty God, our Heavenly Father
Gave prophets to write, and declare of His Word,
Each book, each chapter, and every verse
Words of our Father, to be read, and be heard.

God's word filled with love and compassion
Knowledge, and wisdom, to show us His way,
His blueprint for us, a guide for our life
His Word, His commands, that we should obey.

My book is His Bible, for my choice is His Word
His Word my Savior, Lord Jesus His Son,
All praise, and all glory, to Lord God my Father
My Father, my God, the great Holy One.

The Body of Life

Father, never am I worthy, of your love
This sinful man, you know I am,
Yet through your grace, I do rejoice
To be a child of the Great I AM.

You, my Father God in Heaven
Creator, of all that is, and is to be,
Your spoken Word sent to us as man
Your precious Son, to set us free.

Your Son our Savior, Lord Jesus Christ
You gave, to be our light of life,
His blood spilled, to forgive our sin
His body, our bread of life.

Nourish us, Father, in the body Jesus Christ
In His blood, wash our sins as white as snow,
For worthy are You, of all our love, my God
In me I pray, the light of Jesus will brightly glow.

Jonah

God said Jonah go to Nineveh
Prophesy these words I, have to say,
Now Jonah did not want to go there
So, he arose to go the other way.

Down at the sea, he found a ship
Bound for Tarshish, to flee from God, the other way,
He paid his fare, to sail to Tarshish
To disobey, there was a price he soon would pay.

As they sailed upon the waters
A mighty storm, God brought to them,
Jonah knew the storm was God's fury
He knew how to save the ship, and save the men.

This storm upon the waters
This great tempest, in the sea,
Because I disobeyed my God
This fury, from my God, is meant for me.

Cast me to the waters
That it may calm the raging sea,
This mighty storm, from my God
Not meant for you, but meant for me.

Cast into the waters
A great fish came to swallow him,
Three days in its belly
His price, to pay the payment for his sin.

Then prayed Jonah to the Father
While in the bell at the fish,
With his voice, a sacrifice of thanksgiving
God set Jonah on dry land, from the belly of the fish.

Arise and go to Nineveh
To Jonah, God spoke again these words,
Preach to the people, of that great city
Preach these words, that they be heard.

Then Jonah, journeyed to Nineveh
To preach the Word of God, that came to him,
Nineveh in forty days shall be overthrown
Lest ye repent the evil of your sin.

The people believed God's Word
In sackcloth, and in ashes, they did repent,
They cried out in prayer, to Father God
God' plan for their destruction, the Father did relent.

But anger still filled Jonah
That God gave His mercy, to Nineveh,
Thought Jonah, they should be punished
It was Jonah's judgment, for the city Nineveh.

What message is there for me in Jonah
Is it not to hear, and heed, the Father's Word,
Be not yourself, the judge of others
Judgement will come through the Father's Word.

Always be attentive, to Father God his Word
Any anger in your heart, let it go and do repent,
For from Lord God our Father
His Word, our Savior, Lord Jesus Christ was sent.

Follow not, the way of Jonah
When God asks, for you to do his wish,
Obey, put all your faith, and trust in Him
That you not smell, like some old fish.

A Special Place

There is a place, all filled with love
A place through Christ, there is no sin,
Where Jesus Christ, does call to all
With open arms, to bring us all to Him.

Therein this place, our living God
Who gave His Son, that we might live,
Bled on His cross, to remit our sin
Died on that cross, newborn life to give.

This place, the Kingdom of my God
Evermore, no sorrow, and no sin,
Eternal life, with God through Jesus Christ
Arise my soul and follow Him.

A holy place, of Lord my God
To see His face, creator of all that is,
A special place, that has no end
Forevermore my soul, be only His.

Lord Jesus, hear my prayer
My door to God open up, allow me in,
Judge me, who kneels before your throne
Forgive my soul and guide my soul to Him.

J. E. S. U. S.

J - Is the Justness of my Father
E - Is the Everlasting love, that is His Name
S - Is my Savior, Lord of mercy
U - Is Unchanging, Understanding Grace, He gives to me each day
S - Is Salvation in God's Son, our only way

Put them all together, they spell Jesus
None higher than Jesus is any name,
The Word, the Son of my God, my Lord, and Savior
He saved my soul, to follow Him.

In Jesus only, is my Salvation
Forgiveness of my sins, the reason Jesus came,
His Blood, His death, His Resurrection
Newborn eternal life, for His believers
Thank you, God, your Son Lord Jesus Christ has came.

A Leaf! A Life!

A bud upon a branch
A new leaf, it soon to be,
A tree that feeds, life to the branch
To grow the leaf, that's soon to be.

A mystery, yet great beauty
The work of God, there on display,
The bud, that will grow to a leaf
It is the power, of God's way.

A tree, that grows up mighty
Because it's roots, that are so strong,
Roots of life, to bear good fruit
It's, fruit be life, where is no wrong.

Is not our life, the semblance of that tree?
Just as the bud upon the branch, a leaf that's soon to be,
So to the life, within the womb, a person soon to be
God's miracle of life, born for all to see.

Does not our roots, grow deep and strong
Our root, our Lord, and Savior Jesus Christ,
That we may bear for all, good holy fruit
To obey God, and do no wrong, to become His shining light.

Birthday Gift

Your birthday, Lord Jesus, cometh
My mind tries, to find a gift for You,
So many things here in this world
But worldly things, simple will not do.

So, I will give what I am able
My praise, and love for You,
I will ever be forgiving
As I kneel and pray to you.

In my heart, I'll store Your love
To spend on others every day,
In hope, they will see Your light
And then, follow in Your way.

But, Jesus, I think the greatest gift
A birthday gift, that I can do,
Is each, and every single day
Try to become more, and more like You.

Through Life's Storms

When stormy clouds, have gathered
When the wind, and rain, does cause you fear,
With lightning bolts, and thunder all around you
Keep your faith, for Jesus Christ, is near.

Remember the disciples, on their ship
Out on the waters, late at night,
With the stormy winds, and rain around them
With no land for them in sight.

With howling winds, and stormy clouds
Fear for their lives began to grow,
The raging storm surrounds them
Leaving them, with no place to go.

Just as they thought, all was lost
And they thought, their lives were going to end,
When they had left little hope
Upon the waters, a Savior God sent to them.

The Son of Man, The Son of God
Stepped upon the waters, of the sea,
With unending faith, in God the Father
Walked out to them, on the sea of Galilee.

So, when storm clouds gather
Lightning bolts, and thunder cause you fear,
Have no fear, keep faith in God
For Lord Jesus Christ, is always near.

Prayer for Julie

Father God in Heaven
A special prayer I have, to You,
It is my sister, in Jesus Christ
Julie Kean Gutekunst, for her I pray to You.

Lord Jesus Christ, yours is the power
From, and through, our Father God above,
I pray You, come to Julie through Your Holy Spirit
With compassion, and Your healing hands of love.

Grace, power, and miracles
Lord Jesus Christ, these all are You,
With Grace, use Your power, do the miracle
That will make, Julie's eyes brand new.

Lord Jesus, You, are the Word
That made all that is and is to be,
Show favor to my sister Julie
Touch her eyes, that she may see.

Give complete, and total healing
To her eyes, Lord Jesus, made by You,
Once again Lord Jesus, touch those eyes
Make them whole, and completely new.

Your servant my sister Julie
Many, many prayers she has gave for me,
In prayer, she is always there for others
Hear my prayer, heal her eyes, so she may see.

Lord Jesus, You are the healing well of life
Pure Blessed healing waters, flow from You,
Wash away all afflictions, from Julie's eyes
Gives eyes filled with brightness, eyes that are all new.

Lord Jesus, You are the power
Your loving kindness shows our way,
Please, heal my sister Julie's eyes
A miracle to Your Glory, show Julie on this day.

I thank You, my Lord Jesus
To listen to the prayer, to You I pray,
You are the loving, healing, living God
Make Julie's eyes, to see, shine, and sparkle every day.

AMEN! AMEN! AND AMEN!

Prayer for Barb

Heavenly Dear Father
On my knees, I pray to You,
For my sister, in Lord Jesus
Barb Van Rams Horst, for her I pray to You.

As Your child, she is Your servant
Lord Jesus, she shows a special love for You,
A malfunction, in her system
I bring in prayer, her affliction for You to view.

I pray Your eyes, filled in love
Look and see, the cause of Barbara's ills,
Lord Jesus, almighty healing power is all Yours
I pray to heal Barbara, is Your will.

Lord Jesus Yours, is unending power
You have healed the sick, the lame, the blind,
I pray Lord Jesus You, look deep inside
The cause of Barbara's illness You will find.

Lord Jesus, You are the Word, the Son of God
All things that are, are because and are of You,
Please, Lord Jesus, be the Word
That heals Barb's system and makes it as brand-new.

Doctors, say her immune system, attacks her body
Please, Lord Jesus, place Your loving shield within,
Divert each, and all attacks
So, good health returns to Barb again.

Three in One

It is God's thought
His Word does make it so,
His Holy Spirit comes to teach us
Godly ways, we need to know.

It is God's, Holy Trinity
Our Father God, the Holy One,
The Word, His Son our Savior
The Holy Spirit, all three in One.

Eternally, before the start of time
God, the Son, the Holy Spirit, are all there,
Yesterday they're there, today they're here with us
If there be tomorrow, the Holy Trinity is already there.

Jesus died a sacrifice for us
To forgive our sin, that we might live,
God the Father, Jesus Christ His Son, and the Holy Spirit.
God's Trinity upon the cross, gave all that they could give.

Risen from the tomb
Jesus now at God's right hand,
His Holy Spirit sent for us
To be born again, in Jesus Christ we stand.

If Not for God

If not for God, where were the stars
That shine like diamonds, in the night.
If not for God, where were the moon
Through night's darkness gives us light.

If not for God, where were the trees
That majestically, grow so high.
If not for God, where were the birds
That soar on wings, up in the sky.

If not for God, where were the grass
The lovely fields, of emerald green.
If not for God, where were the flowers
With such beauty, to be seen.

If not for God, where were the beast
That roam, upon the plains.
If not for God, where were the clouds
To nurture life, with needed rains.

If not for God, where were the seas
Waters oh so blue, and oh so deep.
If not for God, where were the corn
The fields of food, for men to reap.

If not for God, where were the man
All brothers, that we be.
If not for God, just think about it
There would be, no you and me.

If not for God, where were the heaven
The kingdom, of my God above.
If not for God, who would it be
That fills my life, and heart with love.

Guard Your Mouth

To earth, fell an angel
To deceive, destroy, and kill.
Lucifer, the Devil, Satan
Turned away from God, and the Father's will.

Though he be a spirit, and cannot be seen
With no body, he cannot speak a word.
He seeks, an open door in our mind
To use our mouth, so he might be heard.

We are sometimes, completely unaware
That Satan's thoughts are even there.
Our mouth, then speaks his evil thoughts
Gossip, and hurtful words, causing others to despair.

He has no key but looks for unlocked doors
Where he may enter, and leave his word.
So, pray to God, in your mind, all doors be locked
That from your mouth, Satan's word will not be heard.

From His Cross Love

When sinful ways, from my past
Come back, and try to fill my mind,
My thoughts, then turn to Jesus
On His Cross, my Lord, and Savior, oh so kind.

Thoughts of evil, from my youth
From long ago, things filled with sin,
Memories, of sinful ways, and deeds
My mind, makes me see again.

My mind sometimes invites me to go back
To see, and do, those things again,
But, my thoughts, go back to Jesus on His Cross
And the sacrifice, paid by Him.

There is evil, all around us
It's around us every day,
It tries so very hard, to draw us in
To then, follow evil ways.

If sin from our past tries to call
Remember not that sin, don't let it in,
Jesus looks down on us, with love from His Cross
As He suffers, for our sin.

From My Heart

Lord God, my Father in heaven
Comes this day, from You all new.
Thank You, for the privileged blessing
This day I start with You.

At the dawn, as the sun comes up
As I awake, to the glory of Your light.
It is my privilege, to pray to You
Who kept me safe, through the darkness, of the night.

I ponder in my mind, words of praise
My words be insufficient in my mind.
To praise Your glory, oh Lord my God
Who blesses me with love, that is so kind.

Holy Spirit speak not the words of my mind
Speak the words, words from my heart,
Words of praise, that give glory to my God
Who has loved me, from the start.

Father from my heart, my love for You
Your calmness ever frees my mind,
Your love does give my soul Your rest
Through Your Spirit, please, Father, make me kind.

When Lord Jesus comes, to take me home
When I'm brought to kneel, before Your throne,
I pray all my sins, be not remembered
And to Your kingdom, I'm welcomed home.

Love and Glory

Father draw close, Your ear to me
From my heart, hear my prayer to You,
Of the things, I need and want
Nearer to You, is my want, my need be only You.

What joy, and glory, in You my God
Your love, and blessings, to me each day,
Your Son Lord Jesus, life's perfect light
Your Holy Spirit, that leads my way.

Almighty Power, with great beauty
In Your presence, oh Lord my King,
All creation, in the power of Your Word
To Your glory, Lord God we sing.

Pure everlasting love are You, my God
To send Your Son, that I might live,
To die for me, upon a wooden cross
Gave all for me, that he could give.

From the Dead You raised Him again
To be seated, at Your right hand,
Belief in You my God, and Your Son, Lord Jesus Christ
I'm born again, in the Son of Man.

A Wish?

If I had, but one single wish
I set and wonder, what that wish would be,
Would I wish, for fame and glory
That all would come and follow me.

Would I wish, for gold and silver
With diamond rings, upon my hands,
With clothes, of finest silk
And many mansions, upon my land.

Perhaps I would wish, to be a wise old owl
To look down from my perch, up in the tree,
To watch, how things unfold each, and every day
And what effect, these things have on me.

Maybe I would wish, to be a mighty lion
With a mighty roar, to strike fear in all,
My kingdom would be all the jungle
A mighty roar would be my call.

Or I might wish, to be a whale
That swims, and roams, from sea to sea,
A huge, but gentle giant
To play amid the waves, forever to be free.

Alas, I ramble on, about a wish
A wish is but a thought, a hope for something good,
A wish is born of fairy tales
To wish upon a star, I've never understood.

Instead of a wish, pray to Father God
Lay all your sins, before Lord Jesus Christ
God's Son,
Ask Him for forgiveness
His blood, upon His cross, newborn life for us
He won.

Through Jesus Christ, give prayer to Father God
Jesus Christ is our hope, for all that is good,
On bended knees, prayers spoken from our heart
Through Jesus Christ, to Father God, are always understood.

Be ever humble, to Father God
You need not be something else, be what God made you,
One distinct, and unique person
In you, God made a special person, one who is all new.

The Cup of Life

I kneel, before a wooden cross, look up and wonder why
A man who had no sin nailed to a cross,
Then in my heart, He tells me why
I came to save you from this death, instead of you, hang I.

Your sin o' man runs very deep, your sin you must repent
The blood spilled from my wounds, for you a sacrifice,
Come drink of life, here from my cup, it's all I have, to give
Upon that cross with Jesus, let all my sin there die.

Amazing Grace flows in His blood, to wash away my sin
Upon His cross His life He give, His life that I might live,
The Father's will be done, His will, His Son should die
Once for all a sacrifice, Jesus gave all that He could give.

His cross reminds us, of His love for us
His life, to pay the ransom for our sin,
I now drink from His Cup of Life
The sinful man, that once was me, died on that
Cross with Him.

For My Great Grandsons

Bring close your little children
Lift them up, to set upon your knee,
Tell them, of Lord Jesus
God's Son, who came to set us free.

Tell them of a baby, born in Bethlehem
On a cold December night,
A hay-filled manger, for a bed
A star above Him, shining bright.

Jesus Christ, His Holy name
God's Word, His one begotten Son,
Jesus is love, and life, filled with kindness
From Father God, Lord Jesus Christ has come.

God sent to us, Lord Jesus
That we should listen, and be good,
To be friends, with one another
Great fun, for all those who would.

Show them sin is bad, not something good
Jesus died upon a cross, for bad things we have done,
Tell Jesus, and apologize, for what we did
He will forgive and forget, so we may live the life to come.

Explain that God gave life again, to His Son
Believe in Him, new life we live in Him,
Forevermore to shine, as brightly as His Son
In God's eternal kingdom, live there with no sin.

Born Again

Once I walked in darkness
Separated from my Lord, because of sin,
A carnal life filled with lusts
Until the day, I was born again.

The old man filled with sin, and lusts
He was alive, and still in sin,
But a new baby Christian
In my spirit, has moved in.

The old man of flesh hates the babe
The Christian babe, that lives within,
The old man of flesh would like to kill him
So, he could return, again to sin.

When the Christian babe, is hungry
The old man tries, to keep the babe's food away,
The babe feeds himself, on God's Word
Breath comes from God, as the babe, does learn to pray.

Every day, the babe grows stronger
As he eats more, and more, of God's Word,
With every prayer, his breathing does increase
The old man growing weak, as God's Word is heard.

The Word of God is wholesome food
For the babe, to grow inside,
To become alive, in Jesus Christ
The old man of sin must be crucified.

In the middle of the night, while fast asleep
The Holy Spirit sometimes comes to waken me,
With God's Word, to feed the babe
Then in prayer, he can freely breath.

Each day, as I awake, in God's Grace
The old man of sin, I crucify,
Then the Holy Spirit can lead me by the hand
For the old sinful man, that once was me has died.

Let It Be Love!

The man from God, Lord Jesus Christ
The Prince of Peace, the King of Kings,
A man of love, who had no sin
Gave of Himself, so we might live again.

The Son, of the Almighty, highest, only God
Lord Jesus Christ, the Son of man,
Spoke of love, with Amazing Grace
In Father God, the holy, Great I am.

What glorious love and joy be in His name
Father God's begotten Son, Lord Jesus Christ,
God's Word, born on earth, as a man
To walk in glory, to be our guiding light.

In Jesus Christ, we walk and live in peace
Upon a cross, His Life for us He gives,
Our sins cleansed in His Blood
Rose from the grave, forevermore He lives.

Believe, reach out your hand, to Lord Jesus
His tender loving hand, to all He gives,
When you give love to others
Through Jesus Christ, in God's Love, you live

Jesus is life, our victory eternally

L O V E

Shared Burden

A child, born with no arms
Love in our hearts does cry out,
Father God, please help this child
God already knows, and what his life will be about.

A life for God to nurture
To live the life, the Father gives,
A life to shine, in God's glory
God's love to show his different, way to live.

God's loving patience, as the child grows
His handicap, God won't allow to keep him down,
God works in special gifts
Upon the child, blessed gifts surely will abound.

Sometimes we look but do not see
For him, we too are in God's plan,
To give him love, from our heart
God works through us, to help the way we can.

Draw him close to you, with a hug
And ask, God, to help him, please,
With no arms, he can't hug you back
But his smile will give your heart, a little squeeze.

Know when affliction, does appear
Let not the burden, be theirs alone,
Carry with them, their burden
Through Jesus Christ, your love is shown.

On Thy Cross

On thy cross my Lord Jesus
On thy cross thou loved me,
On thy cross my Lord Jesus
Thy blood has cleansed me.

On thy cross my Lord Jesus
All my sins laid on thee,
Thy life was my cost
Thy sacrifice paid thou for me.

Taken down from thy cross
Laid in the depth of thy grave,
My soul freed from sin
My ransom Thou has paid.

New life from thy grave
With God, evermore,
At thy Father's right hand
Lord Jesus Christ thy heaven's door.

With Jesus

On the cross with Jesus
On the cross with Him,
Upon His one begotten Son
Father God laid all my sin.

On the cross with Jesus
My place my Lord took there,
Forevermore His love for me
To show how much He cares.

On the cross with Jesus
His life for me He gives,
A never-ending loving gift
His life that I might live.

Within the tomb with Jesus
Lay He there to pay my cost,
Raised to life by Father God
He Lives He is not lost.

Father God we thank you
For the resurrection of Your Son,
Evermore at Your right hand
For newborn life, Jesus Christ has won.

On the path with Jesus
Let my feet walk there with Him,
Then at the end there at the gate
Jesus Christ will take me in.

A New Start

It is early in the morning
A new day, from Christ, has come,
A day filled in God's glory
For those, who seek the Father's Son.

Lord Jesus Christ, the Father's Son
Came to earth, to cast our sins away,
His tender, loving, healing way of life
Our guiding light, to follow every day.

With compassion, love, and humbleness
For our Father God above,
With joy, He fills our hearts, to overflowing
With His forever, unending love.

Through His blood, our sins cast to the sea
To be forgotten evermore,
Our love, and belief in Him gives newborn life
To see what treasures, He has in store.

Our greatest treasure, oh Lord my God
You gave us, Your Son, our Savior, Lord Jesus Christ,
Please, help us to become, the image of
Your Holy Son, who paid for all, our price.

Glory, Love, and Life

Please Holy Spirit take my hand in yours
Let Your loving inspiration fill my mind,
Use my hands, my heart, and soul for Your message
To testify of the Glory of Jesus Christ we find.

The perfect Son of God our Father
A perfect earth filled with pure love,
The word a message from God our Father
The Lamb of God His snow-white dove.

His name Jesus given by our Father
Above Jesus' name will rise not one,
Before Jesus, every knee must bend
To Father God's begotten Son.

His life on earth a symbol to God's Glory
His Word of truth for all to hear,
His sacrifice, His Life for others
In newborn life, Jesus Christ is always near

Look above for the door to Heaven
That door be Jesus Christ the Father's Son,
To be with Father God there be no other
Than Jesus Christ God's Chosen One.

From Him

Stars shining bright
A moon to light the night,
With dawn comes the sun
From God a new day of life.

A prayer given from my knees
To thank my Father God above,
To open up my heart
And receive His pure sweet love.

Holy Spirit please lead me
Through the day that lay ahead,
Let my soul never wander
Your thoughts be mine instead.

Give me patience give me courage
Humble me to my God above,
Jesus be my guiding light
From my heart let me give love.

Lead Your Heart to Love

In this dreary, weary sin-filled world
Of impatience, hatred, and immoral deeds,
Things of this world, and tempting lusts
People do not see or hear the Father's plea.

Let not impatience, be your daily route
Learn patience, from our God above,
While waiting, wear a smile, and not a sneer
Let the Holy Spirit, lead your heart to love.

Hatred, a useless way to use your mind
Let Jesus come, and give your soul a nudge,
Within His presence, a bright new shining light
To let the Holy Spirit, lead your heart to love.

Do not allow immoral deeds, from tempting lusts
Hear our Father God above,
Instead of lust, seek Jesus Christ the "Just"
And let the Holy Spirit, lead your heart to love.

This I See

Sometimes, I close my eyes and try to see
Lord Jesus, walking on a road in Galilee,
His disciples gathered to His side
To hear God's Word, to be set free.

Lord Jesus, sitting on the mountainside
Sharing His tender, loving beatitudes,
The Blessedness, that comes from God
And through His Grace, to begin again anew.

With parables as examples
To light up the mysteries, of God's Way,
To hear Lord Jesus' Words, and ponder them
In things we do, and words we say.

To walk with Jesus Christ our Savior, the Father's Son
To hear, and see this miracle, the Son of Man,
His healing miracles, given through God's Grace
Things you think impossible, in Jesus Christ you see God can.

To know this Man, Lord Jesus Christ, the Son of God
For our salvation, gave all that He could give,
To suffer, and die, upon a bloodstained wooden cross
He died, then rose, so we might live.

Climb Your Hill

As the Holy Spirit guides us
On His path, to guide our way,
He is always there to help us
If something turns our eye away.

Upon life's path, sometimes appears a trial
Some thing, or an event, we did not plan upon,
The Holy Spirit, there to guide us
That on His path we do no wrong.

God's flat path, that is straight and true
Sometimes comes a trial, to test our will,
If we put not our faith in God
That flat path becomes a growing, rising hill.

The path becomes a hill to climb
The Holy Spirit gives us strength, to move above,
He is always there, to hold us up
To move us always upward, with His leading love.

The Holy Spirit will lead us through the trial
He gives us strength, to climb the hill,
It is for us, to reach the top
So, we may do the Father's will.

On the top of the hill, we see a wooden cross
Stained with tears, and our Savior's blood divine,
Upon that cross, Jesus Christ died for us
Now we know, our hill is not that hard to climb

Love

What is love, but tenderness
A special way, to live your life,
To hate all sin and bigotry
To live a life, that's free of strife.

Kindness a gift to give to others
Love them, as you love yourself,
A smile, a compliment, a helping hand
With love, no need for something else.

Clothe yourself, in kindness
Leave bare your heart, for all to see,
The Spirit of the Holy Ghost
Who's love, has set you free.

Father God has loved us first
Our goal should be to do the same,
Love God and one another
To Jesus Christ, give all the fame.

My Cost

Upon a wooden cross
High on a hill called Calvary,
My Savior paid my cost
He gave His life for me.

Not worthy of His Love
Yet it's always there,
Upon His wooden cross
All my sins for Him to bear.

His blood upon His Cross
Wash all my sins away,
A Stone to close His tomb
Three days my Savior Christ to lay.

The Will of Father God
The stone then rolled away,
From death, Lord Jesus rose to life
In His tomb in which He lay.

At God's Right Hand on high
His Love to us He sends,
He loved us from the start
He will love us to the end.

In Jesus Christ is Hope
In Jesus Christ is Love,
In Jesus Christ is Life
With Father God above.

I kneel at His cross
Someday to kneel before His throne,
When Jesus takes my hand
With God, I'll be at home.

A Helping Hand

At night in bed, but not in sleep
Words began to fill my mind,
Words to form this message
A new way to pray, I want for you to find.

Within my heart, I heard these words
You pray to Me, and that is good,
Keep these thoughts, in your mind
A new way to pray, I think you should.

You pray and wait for me to grant your prayer
You know through God, it can be done,
No prayer, to small or big
Given, through your Father's son.

Step forward, with your outstretched hand
In prayer ask Father, can I be your helping hand,
Father God desires for us to be an aide
Give yourself to God, to use the way He can.

Be not just a speaker, of a prayer
Step forward to be active in his plan,
Give all love, and praise to Father God
In Prayer, reach out, and be His helping hand.

Worry

Do you set and worry
About something, or someone,
Worried thoughts, that do no good
Simply work, to wear you down.

As you give yourself to worry
No answer through worry is ever found,
Worry shows upon your face
Through worry, you wear a sad and dreary frown.

Through worry, no problem has been solved
Nor through worry, one will ever be,
All worry does, is steal your joy
To live with worry, it's captive you will be

Don't worry, try to be a helping hand
Pray to God, to do what you can,
The rest, then give to Father God
For all things, are in God's hands.

See your trust in Father God
Take your worry all away,
Praise, and put your trust in Him
Let the joy, of the Father, be yours on every day.

Give praise, and love to Father God
Wear on your face, a smile for all to see,
Worry comes not from God
His message; have faith and trust in Me.

Given

Given from God
Grace, with love so divine,
Forgiveness of sin
Born again life, in Jesus I find.

In Lord Jesus, I see
Your love God for me,
Your son, who died on that cross
To save, such a sinner as me.

Though never, I'm worthy
My God does love me,
His son, my Lord Jesus
Came from God, to save me.

From death, resurrected
Ascended, to heaven above,
To live, with the Father forever
In God's, holy love.

To help me through life
To love all, and do good,
God's Spirit in me
To live life, as I should.

Pure love is our Father
Lord Jesus, the core,
To believe, in God's Word
Gives life evermore.

A Path to God's Garden

Almighty power is the Lord my God
Tender loving kindness is His way,
He, who sets upon His throne on high
His Son, to hear every word, as we kneel to pray.

Jesus Christ, God's one begotten Son
His blood spilled, to wash away our sins,
To be forgiven, to be set free
To be righteous, to Father God through Him.

We look up to the Heavens
Where is God's Kingdom, His domain,
At God's right hand, upon His throne
Sets Jesus Christ, our Lord, our King.

Divine is the Holy Trinity
God the Holy Father, from whom we cannot hide,
God's Son, Lord Jesus Christ, to forgive our sin
The Holy Spirit sent to be our trusted guide.

A shower of God's Blessings
Sent from Heaven, up above,
Brings forth a garden, rich in Glory
A garden filled, with God's pure sweet love

Straight should be the path, to our goal
To see the Father's face. To be at home with Him,
To kneel before Lord Jesus, on his Throne
Our Lord, who removed from us, our sin.

Forevermore to be with God
To learn the mysteries, of His ways,
To sing and worship, the Lord our God
Welcome home, we will hear Lord Jesus say.

The Son

Almighty Power
A soothing hand,
The gift of Grace
The Son of Man.

The Prince of Peace
The King of Kings,
Of Jesus Christ
My heart does sing.

The Word of God
Begotten Son,
Our path to Life
God's Chosen One.

Jesus Christ
Name above all names,
From Father God
My Savior came.

To rescue me
My sins to bear,
Upon His Cross
My sins left there

Divine the Blood
Lord Jesus spilled,
To pay our cost
God's Will fulfilled.

From death, He rose
To life once more,
Our only guide
To Heaven's door.

All praise to Him
Our Risen King,
With thankful hearts
To Christ, we sing.

Eternal God
All Glory be,
The great I am
Who set me free.

To be called home
Before Christ's throne,
Eternal Life with God
Never more to roam.

Star Bright

O shining star of Bethlehem
How bright you light the night,
As witness, to the Virgin Birth
God's Son, Lord Jesus Christ.

High in the darkness, of the night
Your light, beams upon this Holy place,
Born humbly in a stable, on a bed there made of hay,
Our Savior, our Lord Jesus, filled with Love and Grace.

In the darkness of the night
Your light shines bright on Bethlehem,
For all to see and know this is the place
Where is born, the Son of God, the Great I Am.

O Shining Star of Bethlehem
Give Forth Your Light, this Holy Night,
That all may know the Babe, Lord Jesus Christ
Our Lord, Our Savior, our Bright Eternal Light.

His light, that shines so brightly
In our lives, both day and night,
That we may see more clearly
To do no wrong but do what's right.

O Shining star of Bethlehem
Your Light showed bright that Holy Night,
To show the Love of God, for all
In the birth, His Son, Lord Jesus Christ.

Message

As I set here, in the morning
Having read in God's Book, his Holy Word,
I set and ponder, in my mind
To understand, the message that I heard.

The messages, that I hear
Sometimes speak to me, through rhyme,
My desire is then, write down those words
To keep the messages, that fill my mind.

In my mind, it becomes a spoken word
In my heart, to hold it near,
A message, from my Lord Jesus Christ
My Savior wants, for me to hear.

Then upon, some unknown day
An occurrence will cause me to be aware,
The message again will come to me
To remind me, Jesus Christ is always there.

It refreshes me sometimes
To read the messages, that I heard,
To keep my mind, tuned into God
To hear the messages, in God's Word.

Be My God

Before the day, which was my birth
Your loving Hands were there on me,
A heart to fill with love, ears to hear, and eyes to see
Hands, and feet, to do Your will, whatever that may be.

All creation is in Your Word
From you, great favor, I have received,
I ask of you, please be my God
Your child forever, please let me be.

Please Father, in your arms, do hold me near
In your wisdom, so great and vast,
Hear all my prayers through Your Son, Lord Jesus Christ
Please forgive my sins, in Christ my life is cast.

Forever, God my Father
I will obey, the Word you gave for me,
Convict me, when I error
Forgive my sin and let me see.

When I obey my Father, my loving God
His Word, His command, for me to see,
In faith, if I heed, and obey His Word
All things through God, are well with me.

Three Equals One

The New Testament, God's Holy book
A testament, to the glory of God's one begotten son,
The Gospel of Jesus Christ is the Father's Word
Our Savior, and our teacher, of our God, the Holy One.

Born King of Kings, and Lord of Lords
Yet humbly in a stable, He be born a man,
There to sleep, upon a bed of hay
The Holy Son, of Father God, the Great I Am.

Born to a world, filled in sin
Our Savior Christ, our guiding light,
Came to save us, from our sin
To become Righteous, in God's sight.

Jesus Christ, His life He lived sin free
Taught, healed, and called to man,
To put your belief, and trust in Him
To see the Father, in God's Promised Land.

Upon a cross, He gave all for us
To suffer, bleed, and die, on a hill called Calvary,
By evil men, who hated Him
Then three days, He rose again, in eternal life, for you and me.

God the Father, God the Son, God the Holy Ghost
God in Christ, Christ in God, the Holy Spirit in you and me,
In God, they all three be
As one God, they all three live, in you, and me.

Always There for Me

God, you are the center of the universe
You're all that is and is to be,
You're the tender loving Father
Forever watching, over me.

You are there when I awake
You are with me, through the night,
Your loving hand, to cradle me
Through the dark, unto the light.

A loving God, to hold my hand
To guide me safely, through the day,
Your Holy Spirit, in me
To guide my words, in what I say.

A loving God, who's always there
Who knows all my wants, and all my needs,
Your Word, within your holy book
Brings great solace, as I read.

Blessed, is the Lord my God
So gentle, kind, and true,
Forgiving love, with patience
To begin, each day anew.

Your Son, Lord Jesus Christ, to intercede for me
To you, my prayers, for you to hear,
Humbled God, I Pray upon my knees
Your loving arms will hold me near.

The Miracle of a Raindrop

What amazing glory
God puts, in that little drop of rain,
Waters, from the lakes, the seas, the mighty rivers
Gathered high in a cloud, the little raindrop came.

That little drop of rain
Comes from near, and far away,
It travels in a cloud, high in the sky
To fall as rain, along its way.

The little drop of rain
Comes to fill, the living well of life,
The miracle, from Father God
For all His creation, to sustain His creation's life.

God uses then the sun, He made
Ninety-three million miles away,
To shine through, that little drop of rain
To show all, His love for us, with a rainbow, He displays.

Talk

Lord God, eternal Father
I come to talk with you,
I ask, for your forgiveness
Forgive my sins, that I may start anew.

Father as I pray, please hear the words I say
Make clear the answer, to me you give,
Please, Father, guide me through the day
To fulfill your will, God the reason, that I live.

Father God, you're always with me
More, and more, each day you fill my mind,
Each day, as I read your Word
I pray your wisdom, I will find.

Seems God, I'm always asking
For you to come, to help me through,
Please God, hear my earnest prayer
As your servant, how better may I serve you.

I have a silly question, God
But I'm going to ask it, anyway,
Each day, you always do for others
What may I, do for you today.

Humbly, I give my love, my life, to you
By your Son's stripes, I have been healed,
Washed in Jesus' blood, my sins forgiven
Lord Jesus Christ my Savior, Jesus Christ, my holy shield.

For the Joy of a Child

O God, how great the glory
In the smile, upon your young child's face,
The joy, in children's laughter
Shows your gift, of loving grace.

The smile, the children's laughter
An awesome gift, to see and hear,
Jesus, place their smile upon my face
Let their laughter, defeat all fears.

A child's smile, with laughter filled
Life healing power, from our Lord, our King,
A child's smile, God's miracle
May that laughter, forever ring.

Jesus said, to be with him
We must be, as the little child,
Live life, with joy, and happiness
Trust in God be humble, meek, and mild.

How bright the smile, upon the face, of the child
Filled with laughter, from his heart,
With a smile, share his laughter
Each day, an awesome way to start.

See the glowing, loving, tenderness
In his smile, his laughter, from his heart,
God's child's face bathed in joyfulness
In God's love, to never part.

Early Morning Call

When early, in the morning
Before the light of day,
In the peacefulness, of restful sleep
You're awakened, to start a new day.

You try your best, without success
For sleep, to return, again to you,
Listen close, there is a calling
A special thing, for you to do.

The feeling, of loving tenderness
Father God is there, to touch your heart,
To plead with you, to rise, up early
With Him, your day to start.

Rise from your sleep, to thank your God
On your knees, give praise to Him,
In early morning darkness
Jesus be your light, as your day begins.

When called from sleep
Let the Holy Spirit, have His way,
Read, in the Father's book
Holy Spirit, make clear, what God does say.

In the early morning hours
God chose, this special time, for you,
To spend time, to love, and worship, Father God
To start your day, brand new.

Listen

Awaken my soul, my God unto thee
From slumber and darkness, please God, let me see,
Forgive God my sins, forgive God them all
God, open my ears, so I hear your call.

Your Word God, Your Word
Speaks clearly, to me,
Your Word, Jesus Christ
Your Son Heavenly.

Your Son God, my Savior
My Lord, and my King,
My Lord, Jesus Christ
Salvation, He brings.

Divine, be His Blood
That cleanses, my sin,
Resurrected, His life
Now I'm born again.

Lead me, my Lord
Jesus, hold tightly my hand,
Please, let me not fall
To my Father God, in Jesus, I stand.

At the Cross

At the foot of the cross, of my Lord, my Savior
Crucified, lifted high, for all of man to see,
Sacrificed for my sin, Lord Jesus Christ, there took me in
Bled, suffered, and died on His cross, to save me.

At the foot of His cross, I kneel to Lord Jesus
Looking up from this world, my eyes behold Him,
Blood from His stripes, and the crown of thorns Jesus wore
On His cross, my Lord Jesus carries my sin.

At the foot of His cross, a new beginning
God sent His Son, to forgive me my sins,
At the foot of His cross, I am no longer lost
It is there on His cross, my life begins.

May I lift, up my cross, to carry boldly
Let my works, be for those, that are poor, and special needs,
Open my heart to the love, of Jesus Christ up above
Let my heart, and my soul, go where Jesus leads.

Great Will Be the Day

Great, will be the day
The day, that lies ahead,
Great, will be my path
With the Holy Spirit, as I'm led.

Great, will be the day
To receive, the morning light,
Great, will be my day, with God
To do no wrong, but what is right.

Great, will be the day
Great will be the coming night,
My salvation, on the cross
I'm now righteous in God's sight.

Great, will be the day
When I look, to the sky I see,
Great will be, will be my joy
The face of Jesus, looking down on me.

Great, will be the day
When Lord Jesus comes again,
Great, will be the day
When Lord Jesus, takes me in.

Compassion

How great, the word compassion
A word that shows, when loving hearts arise,
With loving, caring, gentle, tenderness
A word of love, to guide our lives.

When storms of life sometimes appear
And wearies those, along their way,
Reach out the hand, of gentleness
With compassion, fill their day.

Be it our goal, to help them
Let our hearts, be straight, and sure,
With compassion, be the helping hand
With compassion, give love, to be their cure.

Our hearts fill with compassion
As we see the sorrow, in their lives,
It is, with complete compassion
We feel the tears, well up, in their eyes.

Let compassion, never leave you
Always keep compassion, as your guide,
In compassion's, gentle, tenderness
You will be always, on God's loving side.

Light

Came a light, to us a guiding light
To light the darkness, in the heart of man,
With glowing love, and tenderness
From Lord our God, the Great I Am.

How brightly shines, this Holy Light
To let not darkness, have its way,
A loving light, to change man's darkness
To make our path, as bright as day.

Truth, with loving kindness
Sent from God, His Holy Word
Light, for us to see His way,
Ears to hear, that His Word be heard.

Great is the light, the light of this world
Great is the light, that guides our way,
With forgiveness, and His loving Grace
Eternal light, in Jesus every day.

In Dark Be Light

Humbled God, myself to you
I come before you, my Lord to pray,
Love, and safety, in your arms
With tender loving mercy, teach to us your way.

Storms, my God, that have appeared
Show how weak, as man we be,
Yet in the storm, Yours is the message
Have faith, and trust in me.

In life, storms may come our way
To cause sorrow, we did not plan,
Yet, as these storms, cause sorrow
God works, to bring out, the best in man.

God works His way, through so many
To help, to comfort, to show His love,
So many hearts, filled with compassion
All coming, from our God above.

Give thanks, to God our Father
Through Jesus Christ, His love for man,
As man, give love, to each other
Through the storm, give aid, to all You can.

Thank you, once again my God
Through Your Son, Lord Jesus Christ,
In life's storms, You are our guiding light
In the darkness, may our light, from You shine bright.

Three Be

Only in Jesus, is God
Only in God, is His Son,
Only the Spirit, together
Holy Trinity, all three in one.

All praise, for Lord God our Father
Who gave for our sin, His Son,
To die on a cross, to pay for our cost
Our freedom from sin, Jesus won.

Our sins washed clean, forever
By the blood, of Lord Jesus divine,
Through Lord Jesus Christ, my Savior
Righteousness in God is now mine.

From the tomb, came a new beginning
God chose, to rise to new life, the one,
Born again life, in Lord Jesus
Comes only through Jesus, God's Son.

Lift up, your heart, and your eyes, to heaven
Seek the face of God, through His Son,
Live in, and follow, the Spirit
For, all three be God, and all three, be one.

Symphony

Your Word, God so wonderful
Your Son's light, that guides, our life,
That teaches love, for each other
To live in love, not strife.

Your Word, God sweet as honey
Sent to us, to show Your love,
Your Word abiding, within us
Pure, as a snow-white Dove.

Your Words, so gracefully flowing
Is as a sound, of music, to my ear,
Each Word, a spoken note, that's played
Becomes a symphony, for me to hear.

Your Word, a symphony, never-ending
In your orchestra, an instrument, I pray to be,
To watch, and heed, the conductor
Lord Jesus Christ, who is leading me.

Jesus the Only Way

O Lord God, my Father
Creator of this body, Master of this soul,
Eternal light, in darkness
Your Holy Son Lord Jesus is He that made it so.

O Heavenly, dear Father
How great the day, how bright the night,
The light of this world, Lord Jesus
Has made us righteous, in His sight.

Our journey God, upon this earth
We travel, on your path, each day,
Please guide us, with your Holy Spirit
That our hearts, and minds, not go astray.

Yesterday, today, tomorrow, You always are the same.
But we of sin Lord my God, in us it is not so,
As we struggled, to find our way
You gave your Son Lord Jesus Christ, our way to go.

There is no path, that is too dark
Nor any mountain, that stands too tall
There is no pit so deep, to hold us in
From Jesus Christ, our all in all.

Lord in me, make all the changes
To be what, and who, you meant for me to be
Forgiver, of my sins, redeemer of my soul
All my love, Lord Jesus Christ, I humbly give to Thee.

Fixed Goal

I pray, through You Lord Jesus
Please hear my words, hear what I say,
My quest Lord Jesus, to follow You
To pray your love, will fill my day.

In love You came, from our Father
A miracle, Your virgin birth,
A shining star, to mark the way
To Christ our Savior, here on earth.

A newborn babe, to lead us
A Prince of Peace, a King of Kings,
As shepherds came to worship
Angels gathered, on high to sing.

All praise, to God our Father
Who sent His Son, that Holy Night,
In Him only, is our salvation
To us, our great eternal light.

Your sacrifice, upon Your cross
Your blood, and life, for us You give,
A forgiving, loving, tender God
So repentant sinners, through your Son, might live.

Lord Jesus, I pray my heart not wander
Help me! That my mind, no longer roam,
My heart, my mind, I fix on You
Till the day Lord Jesus, I am called home.

A Blessed Day from Heaven

Wakened, from the peaceful sleep
God granted me, throughout the night,
A bright new day just made for me
For I am precious, in His sight.

My God, A loving Father at my side
Overflowing blessings, from His heart,
Blessings, filled with love, and joy
Through Him, my day will start.

My eyes God raised to heaven
See skies, stunning so blue,
Clouds drifting by, and birds that fly
An awesome sight, God made by you.

All things we see, we hear, and touch
Lord God, it all belongs to You,
What great beauty, in all these things
We see, God beauty, is really You.

You are the living God
You are the Holy One,
You gave for my salvation
Lord Jesus Christ Your Son.

Thank You, Lord God my Father
For each day, You grant to me,
Thank You for Your Son, Lord Jesus
And Your Holy Spirit, that guides, and comforts me.

Redeeming Salvation

O Lord God, my Father
Creator, my Savior, my King,
Let the love, from my heart
To You, be the song I sing.

On the cross, of my Lord Jesus
Your mercy, forgiveness of sin,
With the blood, of our Savior
Your grace, for all, there begins.

To know God, Your love
The sacrifice, of Your Son we receive,
In Him, our salvation
He who bled and died on that tree.

The Glory of God, Lord Jesus His Son
The redeemer of life, for man, from His sin,
For our comfort, our teacher
The Holy Spirit now lives within.

O Teacher, please teach me
Make God's Word, ring clear as a bell,
That I live, to Lord Jesus
And what I do, I do well.

A Baby Boy

O Holy Night, O Holy Night
O Holiest, of Holy Nights,
O shining star, o'er Bethlehem
O Holy Night, O Holy Site.

A stable stall, a bed made of hay
A virgin birth, there Lord Jesus lay,
A humble birth, the King of Kings
O, Holiness come Angels Sing.

Angels came, there to proclaim
To shepherds, of this Holy birth,
Lord Jesus Christ, salvation's name
Our Savior born, this night on earth.

He's born a Prince, the King of Kings
The son of God, the Great I AM,
His Holiness, the Father's Word
Amazing Grace, the Son of Man.

A baby boy, yet so much more
Light of this world, light of our life,
Our bread of life, His every Word
The well of life, to quench our thirst.

Eat of His Word
Drink from this well,
O praise His name
His story tell.

A Place to Rest

Lord, at the end of day
Comes the darkness, of the night,
Lord, hear my prayer, then lay me down to rest
In peaceful sleep, keep me always in your sight.

In Your arms, I know there's safety
In Your arms, I feel your tender love,
In Your arms, my dreams are lifted
To You, o Holy God above.

Before, the morning light
Before, the break of day,
Holy Spirit guide me, to God's Word
That I may follow, in Christ's way.

Give me place, before His cross
A place, where I may kneel,
To thank my Savior, Jesus Christ
To show the love, for Him I feel.

I received, from Him forgiveness
As He died, to take away my sin,
Then resurrected, by Father God
He is alive, He lives again.

A Prayer for All

May your life, through Jesus Christ, be fruitful
May the Holy Spirit, prompt your way,
May praise be upon your lips
To our Father God, on every day.

May your heart, be soft, and tender
May your words, be sweet and true,
May the love, of Jesus Christ
Shine bright, each day in you.

May the Holy Spirit, be your guide
To help those in need, along your way,
May the Spirit, of our Father God
Be His gift, to what you do, and what you say.

Ever, may you be aware
What Father God expects of you,
Read His Word, and listen closely
It's His Word, that speaks to you.

Heavenly Light

Without You, Jesus, the path grows dim
Unsure my feet, I trip, and fall,
From Heaven, comes eternal light
Lord Jesus Christ, my all in all.

Dear Lord Jesus, as I follow
Please hold my hand, along the way,
That I may travel, Your narrow path
Guide me Lord, so I not go astray.

Your hand of love, You offer me
And You raised me, from the deep,
Lord Jesus Christ, my salvation
Redeem my soul, my spirit, keep.

Almighty is my Father God, upon His throne
At His right hand, His precious Son,
His Holy Spirit sent to live in me
Victory over sin, and death, Lord Jesus Christ has won.

Jesus Christ Be the Glory

To the world, Lord Jesus Christ Messiah
Our Father God's, begotten Son,
Heavenly glory, Salvation's light
Redeeming Grace, Jesus Christ, God's chosen one.

How great the love of Father God
That His Word, be born His Son, as man,
Our guide to life, for eternity
In Jesus Christ, God's will be done.

Our cross, Lord Jesus Christ, did bear
The Father's will, He takes our place,
His sacrifice, to cleanse us of our sins
Belief, with trust, we find glory in His Grace.

Through Jesus Christ, our sins, all are covered
With His blood, never to be known again,
A new life born, to Father God
Through Jesus Christ, our only way to Him.

It Is God's Love

Father God does love me
Though I be, a sinful man,
His Holy Spirit lives in me
In His Son, Lord Jesus Christ, I stand.

Holy Spirit ever present
To guide my feet, to show my way,
God's Heavenly, Holy Spirit
My guiding light, from day to day.

God's Son, my Savior Jesus Christ
God's sacrificial Lamb, for sinful man,
Believing trust, in Jesus
I now live, in God's great plan.

I live for, and by my Father's Word
I listen close, to hear what my Father says,
I must be humble, meek, and mild
To be like His Son, Lord Jesus Christ someday.

When? God's Will!

Ticktock! Ticktock! Ticktock!
The time is drawing near,
From Heaven, in the clouds above
Our Lord, and Savior, Jesus Christ, will soon appear.

Will it be, this afternoon
Or the middle of the night,
Or be in, the early morning
Before the dawn's, new light.

The time, I know not when
My Lord Jesus again will come,
Yet through God's Word, Lord Jesus Christ
I know that day, will surely come.

I pray my Father, upon that day
My Savior, Lord Jesus Christ, will call my name,
With loving grace, and merciful forgiveness
In God's Book of Life, will be my name.

Little Things

The little things, in life
How very precious, to me they be,
All things, from my Lord Jesus
Who my Father, sent to rescue me

The one begotten, Son of God
Born on this earth, the Son of Man,
God's Holy Word, of truth
Lord Jesus Christ, the Great I Am.

Many are great earthly things
Shiny bright today, then fade away,
There is no way, they can compare
To God's little children, in their play.

A smile, upon a child's face
Joyous laughter, how sweet the sound,
To fill your heart, with Jesus' love
When pondered, these little things, become profound.

A tree, with fields of grass
Assorted flowers, to please the eye,
White puffy clouds, in blue skies above
Great, are the little things, made for you and I.

Ten million, one thousand forty, little things
Plus more than stars, that fill the sky,
All loving precious, tenderness
Made, by Lord Jesus Christ, on high.

Great, are the little things
Lord Jesus Christ, who made them all,
Through the love, of our Lord, Jesus Christ
His little things become extremely tall.

Trials

As we live our days upon this earth
There are trials that come our way
Sometimes they seem enormous
And you feel they're here to stay.

They may be trials of anger
They may be trials of fears
They may be trials of things we need
And they bring us then to tears.

As you look upon your trials
As you run them through your mind
These trials that are upon you
You want to leave behind.

Within your mind you do your best
To think these trials away
But then you think they're growing
And you know they're here to stay.

Now step back for a moment
See these trials a different way
They're trials not meant to punish
But to lead you to God's way.

You see that you're not able
To solve these trials on your own
So give your trials to Jesus
As he sets upon His throne.

When trials come upon you
And you cannot understand
Just raise your eyes and look above
There's Jesus, reaching out His helping hand.

Trials are brought before you
Not to cause you any pain
But show to you there is a way
And Lord Jesus is His name

For every trial that comes along
Let your faith in God then grow
Make Father God your all-in-all
His great love for you He'll show.

Know that it is Father God
Who created everything
So in your trials have faith in Him
And He'll be your everything.

Take your trials and call on God
Put your faith all in His hands
It is then through God's great grace
Those trials no longer stand.

A Closing Thought

May God cast special blessings upon you. I hope you have enjoyed these poems as much as I have enjoyed the Spirit working through me and guiding me.

Acknowledgements

A special thanks to my daughter, Jean Kuhn, through her loving work made publishing this book possible.

A special thanks to my spiritual family, Faith Church, Dyer, Indiana campus.

God bless,
Gerald M. Allen

Printed in the USA
CPSIA information can be obtained
at www.ICGtesting.com
LVHW022229301124
797922LV00001B/74